ESSEX COUNTY DEEDS
1678-1681

ABSTRACTS OF
VOLUME 5
COPY BOOKS
ESSEX COUNTY
MASSACHUSETTS

ESSEX SOCIETY OF GENEALOGISTS, INC.

HERITAGE BOOKS

AN IMPRINT OF HERITAGE BOOKS, INC.

Books, CDs, and more—Worldwide

For our listing of thousands of titles see our website
at
www.HeritageBooks.com

Published 2008 by
HERITAGE BOOKS, INC.
Publishing Division
100 Railroad Ave. #104
Westminster, Maryland 21157

Other books by the author:

*Essex County Deeds, 1639-1678, Abstracts of Volumes 1-4
Copy Books, Essex County, Massachusetts*

CD: The Essex Genealogist, Volumes 1 and 2 (1981-1982)

The Essex Genealogist, Volumes 1-24 (1981-2004)

The Essex Genealogist, Index to Volumes 1-15 (1981-1995)

The Essex Genealogist, Index to Volumes 16-20 (1996-2000)

International Standard Book Numbers
Paperbound: 978-0-7884-4543-9
Clothbound: 978-0-7884-7720-1

With special thanks to:

Essex County Registry of Deeds

And volunteers:

Virginia Basken
Richard Ebens
Marilyn Fitzpatrick
Polly Furbush
Nancy Hayward
Shirley Orr
Barbara Poole

Although every effort has been made for accuracy by the volunteers, any deed of interest should be verified by consulting the original copy books.

Essex Society of Genealogists, Inc.
P.O. Box 313
Lynnfield, MA 01940
www.esog.org

EDWARD TAYLOR to HANANIAH PARKER and JOHN TOWNSEND - (5:1) Edward Taylor of Redding sold to Hananiah Parker and John Townsend for consideration of a valuable sum to him & now wife, Elizabeth, secured by Hananiah Parker & John Townsend to be paid yearly during natural life, farm lying & being within the town of Lynn, being two hundred acres upland & meddow, bounded on southwest with land of Mr. Holihock. & on southeast and northeast with great meddow with all ye points & spunge of meddow and islands there to adjoining being part of sd farm & bounded northerly with meddow of Isaack Hart & Edward Hutcheson to ye line y^t parts Lin & Reding & soe along y^t line to ye upland of Edward Hutchenson & soe along westerly to ye meddow of Nicholas Browne & from thence to a spruce tree y^t is marked in ye swamp, & soe along southerly to a marked tree between Major Holihock & Edward Tailor. *Signed:* Edward Tailer [mark]; Elizabeth Tayler [mark]. *Date:* 1 June 1675. *Witnesses:* William Cowdry; Nathaniell Cowdery and possession given according to law in presence of John Person [mark]; Isack Hart [mark]. *Recorded:* 30:6:1678.

JOHN ENDICOTT to WILLIAM BROWNE, Jr. – (5:3) John Endicott of Salem sold to William Browne, Jr. of Salem for consideration of 36 pounds sterling, 160½ rods or poles of ground which is about one acre lying in length east & west 17 rods, in bredth north & south 9½ rods lying, and situate in ye town of Salem bounded on ye east with a lane that runs from north river to the corner of Mr. Browne Sr's orchard and on north and west with ye land of his honored father Mr. Zarubabell Endicot & on south with land of John Preist. *Signed:* John Endecot. *Date:* 14 August 1678. *Witnesses:* Charles Redford; William Murray. *Acknowledged:* 14:6:78. *Recorded:* 31:6:1678

MARY PORTER to THOMAS GARDNER ye younger – (5:5) Mary Porter, relict & Executrix of last will of John Porter, deceased, deeded Thomas Gardner the younger for divers good causes & consideration of good will and affection she bore to loving kinsman & nephew Thomas, son of Thomas Gardner, husband of Mary, her daughter, a parcel of land approx 1½ acres in town of Beverly which her husband bought of Wm. Dixy, bounded by land of Hugh Woodberry, the land of Wm. Dodg on other side, & way by the seaside on other side. *Signed:* Mary Porter [mark]. *Date:* 28 June 1678. *Witnesses:* Thomas Gardner senior; John Higgenson, Jr. *Acknowledged:* 28:4mo:78. *Recorded:* 31:6mo:1678.

WILLIAM LONGSTAFF to MOSES EBONE – (5:7) William Longstaff (cordwinder) of Salem to Moses Ebone of the same town for valuable consideration (provided that if William Longstaff cause to be paid the full and just sum of ten pounds in money to Moses Eborne at or before the 24th of June 1681 sale to be voyde and of none effect) all his part of dwelling house he dwelt in with ground adjoining or belonging thereto which house he lately built & sold one-half of house & ground to Benjamin Horne, it being yet undivided & the whole bounded by water side easterly & northerly. Southerly by land of John Turner & John Milke, & west with a lane. *Signed:* William Longstaff [mark]. *Date:* 29 August 1678. *Witnesses:* Hilliard Veren, Sr.; Nathaniel Felton. *Acknowledged:* 29:6mo:78. *Recorded:* 31:6mo:1678

GEORGE GARDNER and SAMUELL GARDNER to JOHN SWINERTON – (5:9) Leift. George Gardner (march't), late of Salem & now of Hartford & Samuell Gardner (mariner) of Salem, Joynt Executors of the last will & testament of Thomas Gardner, deceased, sold to John Swinerton, (phisitian) of Salem, for valuable consideration paid in hand, a dwelling house with about 10 acres of land upon which the house stood & adjoining to it, situated & lying in north field of Salem by land of John Pease. Also another 10 acre lot lying in north field by land of Robert Stone, also one more piece of upland containing an acre lying by Strong Water Brook & adjoining meadow formerly of Thomas Gardner deceased, called salt meadow, also a farm containing 100 acres both of upland & meadow lying in the town of Salem by some land of Anthony Needham, also one piece more of upland & meadow containing 20 acres lying in said township by land of the Widdow Pope together with all waies, waters, watercourses, woods, underwoods...as bounded at decease of Thomas Gardner our sd father & also all debts, dues or demands, owing on in any wise belonging to the estate of said Thomas Gardner. *Signed:* George Gardner; Samuell Gardner. *Date:* 19 July 1678. *Witnesses:* Hilliard Veren; Thomas Gardner, senior. *Acknowledged:* 22:5:78. *Recorded:* 2:7mo:1678.

JOHN SWINERTON to SAMUEL GARDNER – (5:12) John Swinerton (phisition) of Salem sold to Samuel Gardner (marrenor) of the same place, for valuable consideration in hand paid, the house & lands of late bought of Leift. George Gardner & Samuell Gardner by deed of sale 19 July 1678 viz: dwelling house with 10 acres of land upon which house stood in the north field of Salem by land of John Pease, also another 10 acre lot in said north field by land of Robert Stone, also one more piece about an acre lying by Strong Water Brook adjoining meadow formerly of Thomas Gardner, deceased called salt meadow also a farm containing 100 acres of upland & meadow lying in township of Salem by land of Anthony Needham, also parcel more of upland & meadow containing 20 acres in township by land of Widow Pope as bounded at decease of sd Tho. Gardner & Also all debts, dues, demands of estate of Thomas Gardner deceased. *Signed:* John Swinerton. *Date:* 22 July 1678. *Witnesses:* Hilliard Veren, senior; Thomas Gardner, senior. *Acknowledged:* 22:5mo:78. *Recorded:* 2:7mo:1678.

JOHN GEDNEY to BARTHOLOMEW GEDNEY & HANNAH & SUSANNA GEDNEY – (5:15) John Gedney of Salem sold to Bartholomew Gedney, his wife Hannah, & Susanna Gedney in consideration of love & natural affection he had for son Bartholomew Gedney & Hannah his wife, and daughter-in-law Susanna Gedney widow, all his farme, uplands & meadow situated & being in the bounds of Salem by Ceader Pond which was formerly granted by town of Salem to Mr. William Clearke deceased together with 60 acres as an addition granted formerly by town to said William Clearke & afterward granted to John Gedney which said farm & 60 acres shall be divided between Bartholomew & Susanna upon the request of either party giving 10 dais notice & division to be made by 2 men chosen...to have said farme & 60 acres with apurtenances thereto belonging to sd Bartholomew Gedney & their heirs & to sd Susanna Gedney & her heirs lawfully begotten of her body by John Gedney her late husband deceased. *Signed:* John Gedney. *Date:* March 15 1677/8. *Witnesses:* Samuell Gardner, Sr.; Hilliard Veren, Sr. *Acknowledged:* 29:5:1678. *Recorded:* 11:7mo:1678.

FRANCES JOHNSON & HANNAH JOHNSON to THOMAS PITMAN – (5:17) Frances Johnson (merchant) of Boston and his wife, Hannah, in consideration of a valuable sume of lawful money of New England, sold to Thomas Pitman (yeoman) of Marblehead, their proportion of land situated, lying and being in ye towne farme sometimes known and called by name Mr. Humphries farme at Marblehead excepting one cowes lease or cowes pit which Frances Johnson granted & sold to Edward Hoeman of Marblehead. *Signed:* Frances Johnson; Hannah Johnson. *Date:* 12 May 1677. *Witnesses:* William Gilbert; John Hayward, senior. *Acknowledged by both:* 12 March 1677. *Recorded:* 4:7m:1678.

JONATHAN HART to THOMAS PITMAN, Jr. – (5:20) Jonathan Hart of Salem, with free consent of wife, Lidea, in consideration of a sum of money in hand paid, sold to Thomas Pitman, Jr. of Marblehead, one parcel of land being in Marblehead adjoining westward with Mr. Ambrose Gales land, southwest with land of Samuel Merritt toward southeast with the common being the fift part of an acre as it is now fenced in. Lidea, wife, released dower. *Signed:* Johnathon Hart; Lidea Hart. *Date:* 28 August

1678. *Witnesses:* Edw. Humphreys; Isaack Eveleth. *Acknowledged:* 4:7mo:1678. *Recorded:* 5:7mo:1678.

RICHARD SHATSWELL to "MY CHILDREN" – (5:22) Richard Shatswell of Ipswich, in good consideration, sold to "my children" all estate in Ipswich lands, houses, goods, cattle, & whatever as follows: to son John Shattswell, houses, lands, cattle & tacklings. John to pay him 124 pounds per year during life, & after decease to pay 30 pounds per year to the rest that shall be living beginning at the elder on to the youngest until he make each of their estates half as good as his own out of this estate. Rebecka ten pounds more than an equal portion. But if wife or other friends have given to any children goods, they may part themselves and sett by & divide the rest of household goods equally among them. But in case Richard goes overseas & return again & see cause to have it again, & lay downe but three pence or the value of it, then all ye whole estate shall be returned to said Richard Shatswell, or in case he should see cause not to go overseas & make demand and lay down the value of three pence it shall return as before, or in case John be disabled his brother Richard Shatswell shall have power to demand & enter in the same manner as though Richard were personally present. *Signed:* Richard Shatswell; & possession given to aforesaid: John Shatswell. *Date:* first of March 1676 or 7. *Witnesses:* John Caldwell; Hanill Bosworth. *Acknowledged:* 16:7mo:1678. *Recorded:* 16:7mo:1678.

THOMAS GARDNER, Senior to GEORGE GARDNER – (5:23) Thomas Gardner, Senior of Salem for valuable consideration sold to my brother, George Gardner of Hartford, CT, a parcel of land in Salem jointly laid out together with his as likewise a parcel bought betwixt us of Mr. Hilliard Veren, Sr. Also all ye meadows thereto belonging, with all timber & other privileges being about three score acres. *Signed:* Thomas Gardner, Sr. *Date:* July 22, 1678. *Witnesses:* Hilliard Veren, Senior; John Gardner. *Acknowledged:* 25:5:1678. *Recorded:* 24:8:78.

JOHN MECARTER to JEREMIAH MEACHAM, Senior & GEORGE HACKER – (5:24) John Mecarter (dyer) of Salem deeded to Jeremiah Meacham, Senior & George Hacker, both of Salem, for consideration of thirty-two pound tenn shillings, his now dwelling house, outhouses with ground thereto belonging & adjoining about sixteen rods or pole of ground lying in Salem towards the bridge or caseway, bounded with ye highway to the southwest, the land of Jeremiah Meacham to ye northwest, land of the Widdow Buffum to the northeast & Robert Wilson to ye southeast. To have house & ground with all shops outhousing ground & fence provided if the thirty-two pound & 10 shillings in good & lawful money of New England is paid before the 20th day of September next ensuing which will be Anno Dom 1679 that then this bargain & sale shall be void & of none effect. *Signed:* John Mecarter [mark]. *Date:* 20 Sept 1678. *Witnesses:* Hilliard Veren, Jr.; Hilliard Veren, Sr. *Acknowledged:* 20:7:1678. *Recorded:* 21:7mo:1678.

JAMES COLLENS – (5:26) Certifies Mr. James Collens have liberty to depart with his sloope *Dilligence* from this harbour bound for Salem or Boston, he having entered & cleared said sloope according to custom. By order of the Governor Nantuckett 10:8:78. John Gardner. *Recorded:* 10:9mo:1678.

JOHN COGSWELL, Junior & MARGARET COGSWELL to PHILLIP CROMWELL – (5:27) John Cogswell, Junior of Ipswich with the free consent of his wife Margaret, for consideration of 22 pounds in silver, deeded to Phillip Cromwell of Salem a piece of saltmarsh consisting of 16 acres situated in the township of Ipswich & part of that piece of marsh which has been & still is letten unto Goodman Story of Ipswich being a piece of marsh appertaining to the farm John Coggswell of Ipswich hath upon lease letten unto him for the time of 1000 years by the town of Ipswich, said piece being bounded as follows: upon Chabaco bridge river on the northwest side, upon the neck that runs up the old saw mill ranging along northeast, on the southwest upon a cove coming out of the maine river running to the old mill creeke. *Signed:* John Cogswell; Margarett Cogswell. *Date:* 2 Oct 1676. *Witnesses:* Henry Bennett; John Cromwell; Richard Croade. *Acknowledged:* 16:7mo:78. *Recorded:* 21:7mo:78.
It is agreed that if 22 pounds in silver is paid before last day of Oct 1681 with interest of 20 pence per pound in silver annually until extent of said time & after that rate of 20 pence per pound for interest upon interest in case Cogswell doth any year fail during sd term until time extended until last day of Oct 1681 be expired & then upon that day John Cogswell paying unto Cromwell in Salem at his house principal being 22 pounds with interest, sale shall be voided. *Signed:* Philip Cromwell. *Witnesses:* Henry Benett; Richard Croad.

ELEAZER HATHORNE to GEORGE KEASER – (5:30) Eleazer Hathorne of Salem for consideration of 150 pounds current money to the payment to be made, bound himself to George Keaser. Condition of obligation was that if Eleazer Hathorne or any person claiming under him disturb George Keaser in possession of land sold by within deed then above obligation to be void. Above obligation refers to deed recorded *Book 3d Foll. 164. Signed:* Eleazer Hathorne. *Date:* 25 July 1678. *Witnesses:*

Elizer Keyser; Benjamin Keyser. *Acknowledged:* 25:5:1678. *Recorded:* 8:8:78.

JOSEPH PORTER to HILLARD VEREN, Jr. – (5:31) Joseph Porter of Salem for consideration of 40 pounds in money – 40 rods of ground as per deed of sale with these bearing date appears, sold to Hillard Veren, Jr. of Salem, certain piece of land lying in Salem containing about half an achor bounded with the land of Mr. William Brome to the east, George Kesor to south, with highway to the north & west. *Signed:* Joseph Porter. *Date:* Sept 17 1678. *Witnesses:* Jno Price; Ben. Gerrish; Ele. Hathorne; Israel Porter. *Acknowledged:* 18:7mo:78. *Recorded:* 2:8:1678.

JEREMIA MECHUM, Sr and GEORGE HACKER to HILLARD VEREN – (5:33) Jeremia Mechum, Sr. & George Hacker, both of Salem for consideration of 32 pounds tenn shillings, deeded to Hillard Veren, Merchant of Salem, both their dwelling houses in which they lived & ground on which houses stood & adjoined containing about 1¼ acres belonging to both houses in Salem at the towns end westward near ye bridge or caseway; houses being near together & ground being intire & adjoining each to other & houses & ground lys together bounded with the highway lay southwest ye river northwest with the land of Widdow Buffum northeast & southeast the land of John McCarter. If Jeremia Meachum or George Hacker pay Hillard Veren 32 pounds & 10 shillings at or before Sept 22, 1679 then this sale shall be void. *Signed:* Jeremia Meachum [mark]; George Hacker [mark]. *Date:* 20 Sept 1678. *Witnesses:* John Mecarter [mark]; Hillard Veren, Sr. *Acknowledged:* 20:7:78 by both. *Recorded:* [no date].

JONATHON BRIDGHAM & ELIZABETH BRIDGHAM to SAMUELL RUSSELL – (5:35) Jonathon Bridgham and Elizabeth Bridgham of Boston, for consideration of a certain sum of money, sold to Samuell Russell of Marblehead, one meassuge, tenement or dwelling house with stabe or outhouse with land whereon it stands, land being about ¼ acre lying in Marblehead, bounded by land of John Trebee to southward, house & land of Richard Hanifer lying to northward, & street on westward side. Release of dower by Elizabeth (wife of Jonathan). *Signed:* Jonathan Bridgham; Elizabeth Bridgham. *Date:* 29 June 1678. *Witnesses:* Thaddeus Ridden; Edw. Humphreys (when Mr. Bridgham signed). Henry Russell; Arthur Fursman (when Mrs. Bridgham signed). *Acknowledged:* 16:6:78. *Recorded:* 8:8:1678.

ELEAZER HATHORNE to JOHN HATHORNE – (5:38) Eleazer Hathorne of Salem for consideration of 100 pounds to be paid unto John

Holmes, stood indebted to John Hathorne of Salem & bound himself for payment on condition if Eleazer or any person claiming under him shall at any time trouble, molest, or disturb said John Holmes in the quiet & peaceable possession of that land or part thereof which said Hathorne sould said Holmes as deed bearing date of 4 Dec 1676, then the above obligation shall be voyde & of none effect, or else to remaine & be in full force power & virtue. *Signed:* Eliazer Hathorne. *Date:* 5 Oct 1675. *Witnesses:* Hillard Veren Junior; Ebenezer Gardner. **Acknowledged:** 5:8mo:78. *Recorded:* 8:8:78.

ANTHONY DIKE & MARJERY DIKE to NATHANIELL PICKMAN – (5:39) Anthony Dike (seaman) of Salem, for a valuable consideration, sold to father-in-law Nathaniell Pickman of Salem, every part & parcel of land or whatsoever belonging to Anthony Dike as oldest sonn to father Anthony Dike deceased & surrendered all rights. Marjery Dike wife to Anthony Dike also surrendered all rights. *Signed:* Anthony Dike; Marjery Dike [mark]. *Date:* 11 August 1673. *Witnesses:* Samuell Pickman; William Pickman. *Acknowledged:* 15:10mo:78. *Recorded:* 21:8:78.

THOMAS JEGGELLS to ROBERT GLANFIELD – (5:40) Thomas Jeggells (marrenor) of Salem for consideration of seven pounds, sold to Robert Glanfield of Salem a parcel of land lying in Salem containing about 20 poles or rod of ground, being all that strip or parcel of land that lyes on the east side of land of Robert Glanfield lately bought of Elizabeth Greene to be same length of that land, to be in bredth to the outside of his ground next to the land that is or was formerly Mr. Hardies, except 20 feet in bredth left and served for a highway, or thereabout, running along east side of his land, that was formerly the land of father William Jeggles deceased. So that the bargained primise is bounded on easterly side with said highway & on the western side with land of said Glanfield bought of said Elizabeth & extending so far southerly as land that was sold by said Elizabeth. To have to hold said piece in the use in common with the rest of the proprietors of highway easterly about 20 feet wide. *Signed:* Thomas Jeggles. *Date:* 27 August 1677. *Witnesses:* Hillard Veren, Sr.; Robert Hooper [mark]. *Acknowledged:* 27:6mo:77. *Recorded:* 21:8:78.

JOSEPH FOSTER to ABRAHAM WALCUTT – (5:43) Joseph Foster (husbandman) of Salem for 25 pounds secured to be paid, sold to Abraham Walcutt (husbandman) of Salem, a parcel of land containing 8 acres with a frame of a house. Land lying in Salem, bounded northly by land of Lott Killum, westerly by highway Lott Killum laid out for his own use, southerly with some land of Isaack Goodell, & easterly with land of Zachariah Goodell, having an elme tree for the bounds of the southeast corner which is the corner bounded between premises & Zachariah Goodell at NW corner walnut tree between premises & land of Zachariah Goodell & John Buxton at the northwest corner a stake & NW stake at the end of said highway. *Signed:* Joseph Foster. *Date:* 16 October 1678. *Witnesses:* Nathaniell Felton, Sr.; Nathaniell Felton, Jr. *Acknowledged:* 30 October 1678. *Recorded:* 14:9mo:1678.

ZACHEUS CURTICE, Sr. – (5:45) On July 10, 1678, Zacheus Curtice, Sr., of Rowley Village by Topsfield, delivered into the hands of Samuell Fisher of Brantry, Marshall Deputy of Suffolk County, one parcel of upland containing 7 acres 3 rods at south side of his land abutting land of Ensign John Gould toward northeast & is bounded by land of said Curtice on all other poynts upon which land said Samuell Fisher have levied an execution, obtained by Benjamin Thompson by virtue of a judgment granted at last county court held at Bostone, which land said Curtice avouch to be his estate dispose at the day of date hereof. Entered as a causon by him. Hilliard Veren, Recorder. *Signed:* Zacheus Curtis [mark]. *Witnesses:* Abraham Redington; Ephraim Curtis. *Recorded:* 15:9:78.

JOHN TODD – (5:46) Be it known that we, John Todd of Rowley, stand bound to Henry Skerry, Marshall in Essex County for 40 pounds sterling, for which payment we bind ourselves and either of us. Whereas Henry Skerry has levied an execution for 23 pounds two pence to the use of John Godfery, the assigne of William Prichett upon a parcel of wheat in ye sheafe & Indian corn in ye care, which is at present not moveable & that said Godfery hath withdrawn & absented himself immediately upon levying, the condition of this obligation is that if said John Tode upon reasonable demand made shall deliver to said Henry Skerry or deputy to the use of said Godfery the sum of 20 pounds, halfe in wheat & halfe in Indian corne according to bill at price current, as intimated in the execution dated 14 Feb 1666 with the just charges belonging thereto then this obligation is to be void & of none effect, else to abide in full force. *Signed:* John Tod. *Date:* 24 day 8th mo: 1668. *Witnesses:* Anthony Austine; John Lane.
Endorsement on back that he also heard John Godfery tell him that he had received of Goodman Tod more upon this execution & soe on this bill this 23th of 8 mo, 1668. *Signed:* Henry Skerry
More. I Henry Skerry marshall have received of this bill in part ten shillings 2d above written bond with adorsments, are entered as the Marshall Skerry gave me original paper as he said.

JOHN WILLIAMS to JOHN FURBUSH – (5:47) John Williams of Boston, with Jane, his wife, sold to John Furbush (husbandman) of Marblehead for consideration of 20 pounds current money secured to be paid according to bond bearing date herewith, all his dwelling house & land, yard & orchard about it, with well & all appurtenances being at Marblehead which he lately purchased of William Bartholmew of Bostone, merchant. Bounded south & southeast by land of William Wood, & NE with common way and toward north & westerly of land of William Poate. *Signed:* John Williams [mark]; Jane Williams [mark]. *Date:* Oct 31, 1678. *Witnesses:* William Hamilton; William Chard. *Acknowledged:* Nov 1 1678. *Recorded:* 15:9:1678.

WILLIAM DODG, Jr. to Capt. WALTER PRICE – (5:50) William Dodg, Jr (husbandman) of Salem, and wife Mary Dodg, [late wife of John Balch (marrenor) deceased, - administrator of estate of John Balch] sold to Capt. Walter Price, Merchant of Salem, for consideration of 9 pounds sterling owing from said John Balch & 3 pounds paid to William and Mary in hand, a certain parcel of land containing 2½ acres of land (½ meadow and ½ upland), it being ½ of about 5 acres of upland & meadow between said John Balch & his brother Freeborne Balch both deceased. Land is situated in Salem, in the planters marsh so-called and adjoins the sea to the east & northerly & some ground of Geo. Emory to the northwest & some land of Francis Skerry to southeast and southerly. *Signed:* William Dodg; Mary Dodg. *Date:* 20 Sept 1665. *Witnesses:* Robert Lord, Sr.; Robert Lord, Jr. *Acknowledged:* 26:7:1665 by both. *Recorded:* 23:9:78.
At court at Ipswich 26 Sept 1665, William Dodg acknowledged judgment unto Capt. Walter Price of 9 pounds in satisfaction of debt of John Bach deceased, his wife being executrix.

THOMAS TUCK to JOHN CONANT – (5:52) Thomas Tuck (blacksmith) of Beverly, with wife, Joane who yielded her third, sold to John Conant (carpenter) of Beverly for consideration of 16 pounds, a parcel of land, two acres lying in Beverly. One acre upland ground 20 poles in length from the bank northward, & 8 poles broad & bounded westerly with land in possession of Nathaniell Wallis commonly called Christopher Crowe's land, northerly & easterly with land of Thomas Tuck & an acre of sandy ground or meadow lying between the banks & the river running in a straite line down to the river from ye east line of foresaid acre & bounded southerly & westerly with the river meeting with the easterne line of John Rayment's land & northerly close along by the bank, the land in possession of Nathaniell Wallis & with the aforesaid acre. *Signed:* Thomas Tuck [mark]. *Date:* 28 Nov 1678. *Witnesses:* John Bennett; Samuell West. *Recorded:* 4:10:1678.
Addition: Allows John Conant a highway from east corner of Josiah Rootes orchird & down by side of foresaid 2 acres of land between them. *Signed:* Thomas Tuck [mark]. *Witnesses:* John Bennett; Samuell West. The two

persons entered at the bottom did the like to what is contained in these 4 lines, day & year above written.

HENRY BARTHOLMEW to WILLIAM BROWNE, Jr. – (5:54) Henry Bartholmew (merchant) of Salem and wife, Elizabeth, deeded to William Browne, Jr. (merchant) of Salem, for consideration of 100 pounds, a parcel of upland & salt marsh containing 18 acres lying in south field near stage poynt in Salem. Bounded on north with south river & on east with harbor & on southeast land of Mr. Wm Brown, Sr. & on south with land that was lately Richard Hides & a cove, & on west with land of Daniell Rumboll. Provided if Henry & Elizabeth Bartholmew pay Wm. Browne, Jr. at his dwelling house in Salem 108 pound at one entire payment on or before 1 Nov 1679 deed to be void. *Signed:* Henry Bartholmew; Elizabeth Bartholmew. *Date:* 30 October 1678. *Witnesses:* Charles Redford; William Murray. *Acknowledged:* 31:8:1678 by both & Elizabeth yielded her right. *Recorded:* 4:10:1678.

NATHANIELL STONE to WILLIAM CLEAVES – (5:57) Nathaniell Stone (yeoman) of Beverly, with wife, Remember Stone yielding her right, for consideration of a valuable sum of money, sold to William Cleaves (fisherman) of Beverly, two acres of upland situated in Beverly, bounded easterly by land of Wm Clarke & highway, westerly by the town common, southerly by highway & northerly by land of Wm Clarke & common. *Signed:* Nathaniell Stone. *Date:* 1 November 1677. *Witnesses:* Nathaniell Stone; Remember Stone; Cornelius Larcum [mark]; Mordecay Larcum [mark]. *Acknowleged:* 11:10:1678. *Recorded:* 11:10:1678.

SAMUELL FRAYLES to JACOB KNIGHT – (5:59) Samuell Frayles of Linne, son of George Fraile, sold to Jacob Knight of Linne, son of William Knight, for consideration of 30 pounds sterling & a cow at Michelmas next ensuing date hereof, a parcell of salt marsh lying in Rumlye marsh eight acres situated in the town of Linne near unto Foxhill, bounded with upland of Allen Breade northerly, Thomas Newhall easterly, Jon. Witts marsh westerly & Thomas Browne's southerly. *Signed:* Samuell Fraile. *Date:* 12 Feb 1677. *Witnesses:* Samuell Tarbox; Moses Chadwell. *Acknowledged:* 29:9:78. *Recorded:* 7:10:1678.

JOSEPH HUCHENSON to JONATHAN WALCUTT – (5:61) Joseph Huchenson (yeoman) of Salem, sold to Jonathan Walcutt of Salem, for consideration of a valuable sum already paid, 6 acres and 21 poles lying within limits of Salem, part of a farme that was his father Hutchenson's, lying upon north side of land that was Richard Ingersoll's bounded as follows: upon the southeast bounded with a white oak. Upon northeast with a small walnut twig, upon northwest a small red oak tree, upon southeast with a stake. This deed on the other side was owned by Joseph Huchenson 2:10 mo:78. [depicted map as it was in the deed of land mentioned] *Signed:* Joseph Hutchenson. *Date:* 28 March 1671. *Witnesses:* John Putnam; Nathaniell Ingerson. *Acknowledged:* 2:10:78. *Recorded:* 11:10:1678.

JOSEPH HUTCHENSON to JONATHAN WALCUTT – (5:63) Joseph Hutchenson (husbandman) of Salem, sold to Jonathan Walcutt of Salem for consideration of certain sum in hand pd, one acre of upland joining to the deviding line on north side of Jonathan Walcutt's orchard, at the south it is bounded with a walnut tree near the line, it being fouer pole wide, to a stake & heape of stones, on the northeast from the dividing line. & from thence runneth forty two poles in length toward northwest to a stake & heap of stones, & from thence westward fouer pole to the dividing line of Jonathan Walcutt's land lying with the township of Salem. *Signed:* Joseph Hutchenson. *Date:* Feb 26, 1677. *Witnesses:* James Bayley; Mary Bayley. *Acknowledged:* 2:10:78. *Recorded:* 11:10:78.

RICHARD KNOTT to THOMAS GATCHELL – (5:64) Richard Knott and wife, Hannah Knott, grant to Thomas Gatchell all rights, priviledges that belongs with specified deed of sale.
Assignment was indorsed on backside of deed of sale from John Hudson to Richard Knott bearing date 1 May 1674 & which is recorded in foll. 39 in this book. *Signed:* Richard Knot; Hannah Knot. *Witnesses:* John Trevit; Nicholas Picket [mark]. *Acknowledged:* 18:6:75. *Recorded:* 30:4:1679.

JOSEPH HARDY, Jr. to JOSEPH ALLEN – (5:65) Joseph Hardy, Jr. (marrenor) of Salem, sold to Joseph Allen (seaman) of Salem for consideration of thirteen pounds 15 shillings, a certain parcel of land lately bought of Sarah Browne, relic & executrix of James Browne deceased. Situated in Salem containing 32 rods or poles of land. It is next to streete westerly & is to be there in bredth next said street four pole. And to run same bredth backward to land late of John Gedney, Junior deceased, which bounds bargained premises on the east & on northerly side with land lately sold by Sarah Browne, widdow, to Ezekiell Cheevers & by him sold to Hillard Veren, Senior, southerly with land of James Browne, glazier. *Signed:* Joseph Hardy; Mary Hardy. *Date:* 23 November 1678. *Witnesses:* John Bullock; John Pickering, Jr. *Acknowledged:* 23:9:1678. *Recorded:* 12:10:78.

THOMAS BAKER to JOHN CURTICE – (5:67) Thomas Baker of Topsfield sold to John Curtice of Topsfield for consideration of 69 paid to him, by bills, a parcel of land containing 40 acres lying in Topsfield bounded on the east by William Nicholl's land, on the west & northwest by Ensigne Endecot's land, on the south or southeast by land of farmer Porter, now in the hands of some of his sons, and on the north or northeast by cow common, also a parcel more containing of meddow & swamp about fouer acres, bounded by cow common on the south or southeast, by Ensigne Endecot's land on north or northwest & on north or northeast by a river commonly called Ipswich River and on the east or southeast by Joseph Town's land. From a stake by the river, standing between Joseph Towne's land & this, as it is bounded, running up to a poplar tree by ye cow common. *Signed:* Thomas Baker; Precilla Baker. *Date:* 25 October 1678. *Witnesses:* John Goold; Sarah Goold. *Acknowledged:* Nov 22 1678 by Thomas Baker; Elizabeth Baker, wife. *Recorded:* 12:10:1678.

HENRY BARTHOLMEW to GILBERT TAPLEY – (5:69) Henry Bartholomew of Salem with wife Elizabeth yielding her right, sold to Gilbert Tapley (fisherman) of Salem, for consideration of a valuable sum, a dwelling house & all ground adjoining said house which formerly was house & ground of Mordecai Craford, situated in Salem near causeway going over to Winter Island. House & grounds bounded southerly with path or highway that leads to gutt or caseway & runs from caseway to fence belonging to land of Mr. John Higgenson by the spring. And is bounded by gutt & Winter harbor easterly. Northerly bounded with land of John Higgenson or Major Savage. And the bound runs as the old fence or stone wale did runn up to or neere the front of said house. Ye northeast corner of it, and so runs to ye side corner of house on backside of house, and from west end of house to common land. And is bounded on the common land westerly. To have said messuage or tenement containing one dwelling house with said ground containing in said bounds a poynt of salt marsh next to Winter Harbor & the gutt. *Signed:* Henry Bartholmew. *Date:* 15 October 1677. *Witnesses:* Phillip Veren; Hillard Veren, Sr. *Acknowledged:* 4:9:78 & Elizabeth yielded right. *Recorded:* 13:10:1678. *Addition:* It says Henry & Elizabeth have set their own hand & seal, but Elizabeth did not sign.

JOHN LEACH to JOHN BACHELOR – (5:72) John Leach (husbandman) of Salem, sold to John Bachelor (cooper) of Salem for consideration of eleven pound, 10 shillings – 7 pound 10 shilling paid in hand, other four secured to be paid at or before sealing of deed, a certain parcell of land containing 5 acres lying within Salem neere Riall's side & is bounded northerly with some land of Jon. Greene, & easterly, westerly, & southly with land of said John Bachelor & warrant against any person claiming under me or heirs or administrators of John Freind deceased.

Signed: John Leach [mark]; Sarah Leach. *Date:* 29 October 1677. *Witnesses:* William Lake; Thomas Feild. *Acknowledged:* 2:10:78. *Recorded:* 16:10:78.

GEORGE HACKER to JACOB ALLEN – (5:74) George Hacker (fisherman) of Salem, sold to Jacob Allen (cooper) of Salem, for consideration of sixty pounds in hand paid and secured to be paid, all his dwell house with 14 pole or rods of ground belonging to said house & on which said house stood lying in town Salem against south harbour. Said land being on easterly side next to land of William Hollingworth fouer pole & a half at northern end, and 3 pole on western end & neere five pole & at ye end southerly three pole in bredth. Is bounded northerly & westerly with land of John Clifford southerly with house & ground of John Ellwell & easterly with land of William Hollingworth. *Signed:* George Hacker [mark]; Bethia Hacker [mark]. *Date:* 7 Nov 1677. *Witnesses:* John Harbert [mark]; Hillard Veren, Senior. *Acknowledged:* 20:10mo:78 by both. *Recorded:* 24:10:1678.

JOHN RUCK to MANNASSEH MARSTONE – (5:77) John Ruck (merchant) of Salem, sold to Mannasseh Marstone (blacksmith) of Salem, for consideration in' hand already paid, a parcel or strip of land containing about 17 pole or rod of ground lying in Salem adjoining north side of that land formerly sold to Manasses by John Ruck & abuts to cove or water side to east at which end it is 8 foot in bredth & so runs to westward abuting against common land upon Larres hill so called to which end it is in bredth 20 feet and is bounded to north by land of John Ruck. It is agreed that Manasseh Marstone shall set up & maintain fence. *Signed:* John Ruck [Deed says wife signed it & released dower, but her signature is not noted.] *Date:* Jan 21, 1671. *Witnesses:* Bartholmew Gedner; Nathaniel Beadle. *Acknowledged:* 9:5:77. *Recorded:* 26:10:1678.

MARY PORTER to THOMAS GARDNER, Jr. – (5:80) Mary Porter, relic & executrix of John Porter late of Salem, (yeoman) deceased, sold to Thomas Gardner, Jr., husband of Mary her daughter, of Salem, for consideration of a valuable sum in hand paid, a parcel of land containing by estimation 70 acres lying in Salem. Bounded on one side with land of George Gardner, on another side with land of Samuell Gardner on another side with land of Richard Hollingworth & on another side of John Rubton. *Signed:* Mary Porter [mark]. *Date:* 28 June 1678. *Witnesses:* Thomas Gardner, Sr.; John Higgenson, Jr. *Acknowledged:* June 28:78. *Recorded:* 28:10:1678.

JOHN BACHELOR to JOSEPH BACHELOR – (5:82) John Bachelor (yeoman) of Salem, sold to his brother, Joseph Bachelor (seaman) of Salem, for a consideration of 67 pounds 10 shilling: ie 30 pounds sterling & 37 pound 10 shilling in goods, a piece of swamp & upland containing an acre thereabout & 2 dwelling houses in Salem bounded southerly with Royals side, westerly with Abraham Warren's land, northerly with Abraham Warren's orchard & northeast with land of said Joseph Bachelor. *Signed:* John Bachelor. *Date:* Nov 26, 1678. *Witnesses:* Jonathan Wallcutt; Hilliard Veren, Sr. *Acknowledged:* 30:10mo:78. *Recorded:* 29:10:1678.

WILLIAM WILLIAMS to JOHN CONANT – (5:84) William Williams (bricklayer) late of Beverly, now in Wenham sold to John Conant [son of Roger Conant deceased] (house carpenter) of Beverly for consideration of 55 shillings in money & goods in hand paid, a parcell of land lately bought of John Grover, containing about 1 acre & about 3 pole of land; acre being mentioned with bounds in a deed by John Grover dated 27 Nov 1672. The 3 pole being added since the parcel of land lying in Beverly. The acre & 3 pole added to acre lies at the western end next Cott swamp, the whole being bounded with land of John Grover easterly & southerly; with Cott swamp westerly & northerly with common land. *Signed:* William Williams [mark]. *Date:* 2 July 1676. *Witnesses:* Elizabeth Mackmallen; Hilliard Veren, Sr. *Acknowledged:* 2:4mo:76. *Recorded:* 18:11:1678.

JOHN BENETT to JOHN CONANT – (5:86) John Benett (weaver) of Beverly sold to John Conant (carpenter) of Beverly for consideration of 100 pounds, ½ acre & 15 pole of upland ground with dwelling house lying in Beverly. Bounded northerly with land in possession of David Thomas, easterly with land of Edmond Grover, southerly with land of Anthony Wood, westerly with highway or common road. Barn, nursery & half trees in the orchard are excepted. Edmond Grover gives up all right to & interest in ½ acre &15 pole of land [mark]. *Signed:* John Bennett. *Date:* 24 Sept 1677. *Witnesses:* William Elliott; Samuell West. *Acknowledged:* 31:8:77 – Wife yielded thirds (no name); by John Benet; by Edmond Grover 3 Apr 1678. *Recorded:* 18:11:78.

JOHN GROVER to JOHN BENETT – (5:88) John Grover (husbandman) of Salem sold to John Benett (weaver) of Beverly for consideration of 16 shillings, 8 pole of upland ground lying in Beverly & bounded norwest on roadway that goes to Draper's poynt & ye mill northwest, easterly with highway or common road, southerly & westerly with the orchard land of said Grover. That is to say 4 pole in length by country highway & two pole wide by the way as we go to the mill on Draper's poynt. *Signed:* John

Grover. *Date:* 8 August 1677. *Witnesses:* Samuell West; John Leb. *Acknowledged:* 9:6:77. *Recorded:* 18:11:78.

JOHN BENET to JOHN CONANT – (5:90) John Benet sold to John Conant (carpenter) of Beverly for consideration of 20 shillings now due & owing to John Conant, all ye messuage or tenem't & hereditements within mentioned or to be demised, as also his estate right, title & interest of & into same. *Signed:* John Bennet. *Date:* 3 October 1677. *Witnesses:* Nehemiah Grover; Mark Hascal. *Acknowledged:* 3:2mo:1678. *Recorded:* 18:11:1678.

SAMUEL DUNTON to Capt. GEORGE CORWIN – (5:91) Samuel Dunton (wheelright) of Redding with consent of wife, Ann who yielded her thirds, sold to Capt. George Corwin (merchant) of Salem for valuable consideration in hand paid, 60 acres of upland within Redding by Ipswich River. Being bounded on one end with highway and on other end with Andover bounds, & on northeast side land of Peter Palfery lately deceased, & on other side of land of ... [blank]. *Signed:* Samuel Dunton [mark]; Ann Dunton. *Date:* 4 October 1665. *Witnesses:* Edw. Norrice; John Higgenson. *Acknowledged:* 4:8:1665. *Recorded:* 10:12mo:1678.

WILLIAM HOOPER to EDMOND GALE – (5:92) William Hooper (fisherman) of Beverly with wife Elizabeth yielding her dower, sold to Edmond Gale (seaman) of Beverly for consideration of 15 pounds, ten acres of upland in Beverly. Bounded easterly with land of Robert Stone, John Stone, Tho. Chubb, southerly with common land, westerly with common land, & northerly with land of Edmond Grover. *Signed:* William Hooper [mark]; Elizabeth Hooper [mark]. *Date:* 23 April 1672. *Witnesses:* Robert Margaine; John Williams. *Acknowledged:* 20:10mo:78. *Recorded:* 10:12mo:1678.

EDMOND GALE to NATHANIELL WALLIS, Sr. – (5:94) Edmond Gale (fisherman) of Beverly, with consent of wife Sarah, sold to Nathaniell Wallis, Sr., late of Casco Bay, now in Beverly, for consideration of a valuable sum in hand paid, bill of sale or deed of land written on other side & all rights to land timber & all other privileges. *Signed:* Edmond Gale; Sarah Gale. *Date:* 10 Feb 1678. *Witnesses:* Frances Neale Senior; Frances Neale Jr. *Acknowledged:* 13:12mo:1678 by both. No recorded date.

EZEKIELL FOGG to JOHN MASTONE, Jr. – (5:95) Ezekiell Fogg (marchant) citizen and skinner of London now of New England sold to John Mastone, Jr. (carpenter) of Salem for consideration of ten pounds of lawful money, a small tract of land lying in Salem near meeting house encompassed on both sides north & south, east & west by land of Mr. John Hathorne merchant, formerly belonging to Ralph Fogg citizen & skiner of London late deceased. About 30 pole or rod of ground & is in bredth facing toward meeting house to east 33 feet, extending backward as far as outward ditch just beyond on orchard westward being in length from ye street or house of said Mastone to said ditch upward of 15 pole, being now in tenure & occupation of Hillard Veren, Sr. Ezekiell Fogg doe grant John Marstone may have premises without trouble or molestation from sd Ezekiell Fogg or heires of sd Ralph Fogg or John Fogg brother of sd Ezekiell Fogg. Sd. Ezekiell Fogg doe oblige himself in sum of 10 pounds to sd Maston to save Marstone undamnified from any trouble or molestation from Anna, wife of Ezekiell in any claim of her dower or thirds. *Signed:* Ezekiell Fogg. *Date:* 25 May 1676. *Witnesses:* Bartholmew Gidney; John Pickering. *Recorded:*13:12:78.

RICHARD HIDE to JOHN MASTON, Jr. – (5:98) Richard Hide (ship carpenter) of Salem sold to John Maston, Jr. (house carpenter) of Salem for consideration of fifty pounds two parcels of land lying at or near Stage Poynt so called in south fields belonging to Salem. One parcel containing 2½ acres bounded northerly with land James Poland, southerly with land of Mr. William Browne senior abutting upon a mill pond westerly & a cove coming in behind Stage Poynt easterly. Another parcel containing 2½ acres bounded easterly with land of Mr. Wm Browne senior, westerly & northerly with land of Mr. Henry Bartholmew, & southerly said cove behind Stage Poynt. *Signed:* Richard Hide. *Date:* 22 March 1677/8. *Witnesses:* John Massey; Elias Mason; Hilliard Veren, Sr. *Acknowledged:* 22:1mo:1677/8. *Recorded:* 4:12:78.

NICHOLAS BARTLETT to JOHN BALDEN – (5:101) Nicholas Bartlett of Salem sold to John Balden (seaman) of Salem for consideration of 57 pounds, a dwelling he built on land bought of the Town of Salem with ¼ acre which house was on. Land lying in Salem, bounded north by a cove, a spot of common land to the east with a street or highway to the south, with a lane or highway down to the cove on the west. *Signed:* Nicholas Bartlett [mark] with wife yielding thirds. *Date:* 10 April 1667. *Witnesses:* Hilliard Veren; Bartholomew Gedney. *Acknowledged:* 10:3mo:67. *Recorded:* 14:12mo:78.

JOHN GINGELL to WILLIAM IRELAND – (5:102) John Gingell (tailor) of Salem sold to William Ireland (yeoman) of Rumly Marsh in Boston for consideration of 13 pounds, all his part of upland & meadow in a farm sometime Richard Bellingham's at Willis hill Salem, part of the meadow on the east side of William Ireland's house commonly called neck meadow & all his part of upland on the southeasterly corner of said farm bounded by lands of Thomas Fuller on the south & land of John Putman on the east. Also, upland at the west end of a hill bounded on the south by a pond, easterly & westerly by Bray Wilkenson's & north by Aron Wayes & said Ireland's land. *Signed:* John Gingell. *Date:* 6 February 1678. *Witnesses:* Thomas Robbins; George Dean. *Acknowledged:* 19:12mo:78. *Recorded:* 20:12mo:78. *Addendum:* William Ireland acknowledged that half of lot at western end of ye hill as it is bounded in ye deed is Aron Waye, Junior & William Waye's. *Signed:* Wm. Ireland, Sen'r.

WILLIAM LORD (the younger) to EDWARD FLINT – (5:105) William Lord, the younger, (husbandman) of Salem sold to Edward Flint (husbandman) of Salem for consideration of 15 pounds 10 shillings, one acre of land in Salem, bounded with street or highway to the south, the ground of Henry Reynolds to the west, by land of Robert Buffum on the north & by land of said Edward Flint to the east. *Signed:* William Lord; Jane Lord [mark]. *Date:* 8 June 1664. *Witnesses:* Hilliard Veren; Phillip Veren. *Acknowledged:* 29:2mo:67. *Recorded:* 5 March 78.

Widdow ELIZABETH SPOONER to EDWARD FLINT – (5:107) Widdow Spooner of Salem sold to Edward Flint (husbandman) of Salem for consideration of 6 pounds by bill, land of 1 acre in Salem bounded with a highway to the east, with land of said Edward Flint to the south and west & with the river to the north. *Signed:* Elizabeth Spooner. *Date:* 8 May 1668. *Witnesses:* William Hathorne; John Simpson. *Acknowledged:* 11:12mo:75. *Recorded:* 5 March 1678.

RICHARD DIKE to JOHN FITCH – (5:108) Richard Dike of Gloucester sold to John Fitch of Gloucester for consideration of 45 pounds, 1 house and houselot with one acre added which was part of lot of John Davis & about 6 acres he bought of his grandfather, Harden of Waymouth, plus one parcel lying between the said six acres and land of Elizabeth Fryer, with both the parcels of meadowground upon the eastern side of the highway leading from Goodman Stainwood's house to the meeting house. The one parcel of saltmarsh ground between the marsh of John Davis & Elizabeth Fryers; & the other parcel of saltmarsh ground joins to the marsh of Phillip Stainwood, Senr's & so to the land of Elizabeth Fryer. The house being bounded with the land of John Davis on the south & the land of Elizabeth Fryer on the north, and a highway both to the east and west. The other two parcels of upland and one of the meadow lies between the land of Phillip Stainwood and Elizabeth Fryer, Fryer's land being on the south and Stainwood's land on the north. *Signed:* Richard Dike [mark]. *Date:* 30

January 1668. *Witnesses:* Thomas Prince [mark]; Thomas Riggs; Rebecca R. Daliber [mark]. *Acknowledged:* 29 March 69. *Recorded:* 10:1mo:1678.

ANTHONY NEEDHAM to EDWARD FLINT – (5:111) Anthony Needham (yeoman) of Salem sold to Edward Flint (yeoman) of Salem for consideration of 30 pounds, 3 acres of land in Salem in a field lying behind the dwelling house of the said Edward Flint, one of the said acres bounded with Broad street to the south, the lane that leads to the north river east, lands of the said Edward Flint to the north and west. The other two acres in the same field bounded to the river north, the land that was lately or now Widdow Buffum's west, land of Hen. Reynolds south, the lands of said Edward Flint east. *Signed:* Anthony Needham [mark]; wife, Ann Needham, with release of dower. *Date:* 10 March 1678. *Witnesses:* Nathaniel Putnam; Hilliard Veren, Sr. *Acknowledged:* 10:1mo:78:9. *Recorded:* 12:1mo:78:9.

SAMUEL VERY, Sr. to JOSHUA BUFFUM – (5:113) Samuel Very, Sr. of Salem, with consent of wife, Alce, sold to Joshua Buffum (yeoman) of Salem for consideration of 7 pounds in silver, 7½ acres of upland & lowland lying at the northwest end of the cedar swamp by the cedar pond in Salem bounded with a forked birch tree by the swamp side on the northeast corner, thence to the pond southwest, bounded with a cedar, and so bounded with the pond on the southwestern side, and from the aforementioned birch tree to a great stone northwest, and from thence to the pond southwesterly, or else to the extent of the bounds of his farm, so much as shall make up seven acres and one-half of land aforementioned, with benefit of a sufficient cartwaye through his land onto land which he sold. *Signed:* Samuel Verry. *Date:* 20 December 1678. *Witnesses:* Richard Croady; Joseph Lord [mark]. *Acknowledged:* 16:11mo:1678. *Recorded:* 20 Mar 1678:9.

THOMAS BRACKETT to PHILLIP CROMWELL – (5:115) Thomas Brackett (husbandman) of Salem sold to Phillip Cromwell (slaughterer) of Salem for consideration of 26 pounds 3 shillings ten pence owed to Phillip Cromwell & mortgaged to Phillip Cromwell, a dwelling house lying in a field called the North field, with the land upon which it stands & 10 acres of land thereunto belonging, bounded by land of John Neale's northerly and easterly, by a highway southerly, by land of John Smale westerly. Above sums of money to be paid at or before 29 September 1678, next ensigning the date and day hereof or when the time is expired & the debt not paid, Brackett to give all his rights & titles in the said house & land to the said Cromwell. *Signed:* Thomas Brackett [mark]. *Date:* 27 September 1673. *Witnesses:* Thomas Ives; Zebulon Hill. *Acknowledged:* 29:1ˢᵗmo:1679. *Recorded:* 2 Apr 1679. Jeremiah Neale & Steeven Small testified they saw

Thomas Brackett deliver Phillip Cromwell his dwelling house by possession & land by turf & twig. *Signed:* Jeremiah Neale; Steeven Small. *Date:* 28 February 1678:9.

JOSEPH GRAFTON to PASCO FOOT – (5:117) Joseph Grafton (mariner) of Salem sold to Pasco Foot (mariner) of Salem for consideration of eight pounds five shillings a parcel of land being half of a parcel of his that lately John Day was possessed of and whereon John Day's dwelling house stands in Salem, bounded by land of John Day as the partition fence now stands to the south, with the land of Edward Woolen easterly, the street north, & with a lane or particular highway westerly. *Signed:* Joseph Grafton. *Date:* 2 April 1679. *Witness:* Bethia Grafton. *Acknowledged:* 13:11mo:1679. *Recorded:* 4 April 1679. Entered as a causion.

PASCO FOOT to ZACHARIAH WHITE – (5:119) Pasco Foot (mariner) of Salem sold to Zachariah White (seaman) of Salem for consideration of 74 pounds his dwelling house with the ground it stood on, being all the parcel of ground lately bought of Mr. Joseph Grafton in Salem, bounded with the land of John Day southerly as the partition fence now stands, betwixt premises & John Day's house, on East by land of Edward Woolen north with a street, & west with a small lane left as a particular highway. *Signed:* Pasco Foot. *Date:* 3 April 1679. *Witnesses:* Benjamin Marston; Hilliard Veren, Sr. *Acknowledged:* 3 April 1679. *Recorded:* 4 April 1679. *Release of Dower:* Margaret Foot gave up her thirds of house & ground in instrument. 10:10mo:1680.

EDWARD FLINT to ANN NEEDHAM – (5:122) Edward Flint (yeoman) of Salem sold to Ann, wife of Anthony Needham with consent of her sd husband for consideration of 20 pounds, ¼ acre of land in Salem, bounded by that broad street that goes to the bridge or causeway at the western end of the town south the land of Henry Reynolds to the west, by land of said Edward Flint to the north and east. *Signed:* Edward Flint; wife, Elizabeth Flint [mark] with release of dower. *Date:* 10 Mar 1678:9. *Witnesses:* Hilliard Veren, Sr.; Nathaniel Putman. *Acknowledged:* 10:1mo:1678:9. *Recorded:* 9 April 1679.

JOHN CROMWELL to BENJAMIN SMALE – (5:125) John Cromwell (slaughterer) of Salem sold to Benjamin Smale (sailmaker) of Salem for consideration of 5 pounds 10 shillings land in Salem fourteen foot square at the northwest corner of his ground belonging to his dwelling house, bounded by street on north, by his land to east and south and to the west by a lane that runs between his land and Mrs. Hanna Brown's, widdow, relict of James Brown deceased, also a right with himself in lane so far as his land ran backward, according to that deed given by Thomas Jeggles to him. *Signed:* John Cromwell. *Date:* 21 March 1678:9. *Witnesses:* Peter Cheevers; Hillard Veren, Sr. *Acknowledged:* 21:1mo:1678:9. *Recorded:* 10 April 1679.

JOHN NORMAN to SAMUEL LEACH – (5:127) John Norman (ship carpenter) of Salem, as admin. of estate of Jno. Norman, Sr. & Anabell, his wife, both of Manchester engaged to deliver unto Samuel Leach in full for the whole that is due to Samuel Leach from the estate of his father, John Norman & Anna Bell, his wife of Manchester, deceased, one acre and one-half of meadowland, one acre of land upon plaine, ¼ & half quarter of upland joining & being enclosed to the said Leach's land lying near the Beaver dam or butting & bounding to the fresh meadows. The aforesaid meadow land is understood to be in the pond land contained in the 4 hundred acres, and also to give to the said Leach an eighth part of the commonage belonging to the estate of the above said John Norman & Annabell, his wife, deceased. This refers to another writing entered on the back side of it & recorded in the book 6 foll. 80. *Signed:* John Norman. *Date:* 15 Nov 1680. *Witnesses:* Jeremiah Neale; Daniel Bacon; Benjamin Gerrish. *Acknowledged:* 17:9mo:1680. *Recorded:* 17:9mo:1680.

SAMUEL ROBISSON & JOHN ROBISSON to SAMUEL GARDNER – (5:128) Samuel Robisson (tailor) & John Robisson (tailor) both of Salem sold to Samuel Gardner (mariner) of Salem for consideration of 5 pounds ten shillings, a parcel of land containing a quarter of an acre in Salem near the dwelling house of William Robbisson, late deceased, on the other side to the right hand of the common road or highway that goes from Salem to Topsfield, being bounded by a little river or brook northerly, with the said highway or common land westerly & southerly, & with the land of the said Samuel Gardner easterly. *Signed:* Samuel Robisson; John Robisson; Martha Robisson [mark]; Sarah Robisson [mark]. Martha, wife of Samuel, & Sarah, wife of John, released dower. *Date:* 19 Nov 1678. *Witnesses:* Benjamin Balch; Hilliard Veren, Sr. *Acknowledged:* 5:2mo:1679 (Martha & Sarah consented). *Recorded:* 14:2mo:1679.

DANIEL EPPS, SR. to WILLIAM BROWNE, SR. – (5:130) Daniel Epps, Sr. (gentleman) of Ipswich sold to William Browne, Sr. (merchant) of Salem for consideration of 135 pounds sterling a certain island in Ipswich containing 60 acres of upland & 40 acres of salt marsh bounded as follows: John Ring's land & part of Mr. Simond's on the southwest, part of Mr. Simond's & Killecrus Rose's land on the northwest, a creek parting along between them on the northeast, a cut through a parcell of marsh on the southeast & south, a creek compassing an island known by the name of pine island, & a river called little chadbrock's river on the south until it comes to John Ring's land again. It is understood that this island, upland & marsh with every part & parcel thereof is to remain in the possession & for the use & improvement of the said Epps or his assigns for the full & just time of five years, next ensuing the date of these presents for the term of which five years beginning from February 6: 1678:9 & ending February 6: 1684:5 & for the use of the aforesaid land, said Epps is by these presents bound & engaged to pay rent unto the said Browne or his assigns the sum of nine pounds per annum in current money of New England to be delivered at the town of Salem unto the said Browne or his assigns. It is further understood that if the said Epps shall pay or cause to be paid unto the said Browne or his assigns any portion of the principle within the said term of the five years before mentioned that then a proportionable abatement is to be made of the said rent according to what is received, provided & it is agreed by & between the said parties (Epps & Browne) that if the said Epps or his assigns shall well & truly pay or cause to be paid to the said Browne or his assigns, the sum of one hundred thirty-five pounds in current money of New England & also what sums of rent shall be due according to the promise in Current money at or before the end of the term of the above mentioned five years, that then this present indenture shall be void & of no effect, but in case of the least failure in any kind, then this demise, grant & bargaine to stand in full force & power. *Signed:* Daniel Epps. *Date:* 6 February 1678/9. *Witnesses:* Nathaniell Wells; Simon Epps. *Acknowledged:* 21 March 1678:9. *Recorded:* 15:2mo:1679.

7 Feb 1683/4 whereas Capt. Daniell Epps engaged a parcel of land to him, an estate upon condition by mortgadge bearing date sixth February 1678:9 William Browne acknowledged full satisfaction of the said Epps & delivered up the mortgage aforesaid & quit all claim to land engaged in the said mortgage. *Signed:* William Browne. *Date:* sixth February 1683/4. *Witness:* Benjamin Browne.

JOSEPH POPE to JOHN BURTON – (5:133)   Joseph Pope (husbandman) of Salem, with consent of wife, sold to John Burton (planter) of Salem for a valuable consideration one dwelling house and orchard together with fourteen acres of land lying in the town of Salem in a place called the north field & bounded as follows: on the north side with land of John Pudney, on the south with land of Isaack Cook & Richard Bishop, on the east with the land of John Hill, Job Swinerton & John Pease & westward on the common or highway. *Signed:* Joseph Pope [mark]. *Date:* 18 July 1664. *Witnesses:* Zerababell Endicott; John Kitchin. *Acknowledged:* 1:12mo:64. *Recorded:* 15:2mo:1679.

EDWARD BERRY to THOMAS CLEARK – (5:135) Edward Berry (mariner) late of Salem, now of Marblehead, as attorney for son, Edward, acknowledged receipt of 56 pounds from Thomas Cleark due by bill bearing date of 18 October 1677, being lost but entered upon records & release quitclaim Thomas Cleark from all causes of action. *Signed:* Edward Berry. *Date:* 20 March 1678:9. *Witnesses:* Hilliard Veren, senior; James Browne. *Acknowledged:* 21:1mo:7 8/9. [no Recorded date]

EDWARD RICHARDS & JOHN RICHARDS – (5:136) Indenture made 18 June 1673 between Edward Richards (joyner) of Lynn & John Richards (husbandman) of Lynn, his son. Edward Richards in consideration that John Richards is his beloved son & hath acquit & discharge John Richards from any satisfaction as touching the underwritten premisses that given & made over unto John Richards & with consent of Ann, his wife, 1 parcel of upland in Lynn, 20 acres caled Mulliner's lot bounded on S side with lands of Josiah Winter, east by a run or smale brooke, butting north upon comon & Mr. King's land & west upon highway that goeth to Marblehead, to have premisses unto John Richards & his heires if John Richards have any lawful issue, either male or female, if not then it shall return again & be in power of John Richards to give it unto any of his brothers or sisters after the decease of his wife but not to be given to any other but unto ye name of ye Richards if any survive or elce to next of kin of him. *Signed:* Edward Richards [mark]. *Witnesses:* John Hathorne; Ralph King. *Acknowledged:* 23:5mo:75. *Recorded:* 23 Apr 1679.

EDWARD FLINT to JOSHUA BUFFUM & CALEB BUFFUM – (5:138) Edward Flint (yeoman) of Salem sold to Joshua Buffum (yeoman) and Caleb Buffum (yeoman) both of Salem, in consideration of 1 acre of land which he lately bought of Joshua & Caleb Buffum or by way of exchange as per deed bearing date with these presents & 40 shillings, 1 acre of land in Salem & is one of three acres of land lately sold to him by Anthony Needham by deed dated 10 March 1677/78, lying on the western side of a partition fence set up the 17 Aprill 1679, by Edward Flint & the said Joshua & Caleb as the renued bounds by agreement upon exchange of the said land being now & also for about twelve years last past in the possession of the said Joshua & Caleb Buffam & is bounded with some land of Henry Renolds south, & the land of the said Flint as the said partiton fence runs east, & some land of Joshua & Caleb west, & abutting against the north river, north. *Signed:* Edward Flint. *Date:* 18 of April 1679. *Witnesses:* Jehoadan Harvey; Hilliard Veren, sr. *Acknowledged:* 18:2mo:1679. *Recorded:* 30:2mo:1679.

DANIEL RUMBOLL to JOHN ROGERS – (5:141) Daniel Rumboll (blacksmith) of Salem with consent of wife, sold to John Rogers (glazier) of Salem for consideration of 30 pounds, one quarter acre of land in Salem next to the dwelling house of the said Daniel Rumboll, bounded on the east with land of Robert Wilkes, westward with land of Mr. John Higgenson, Jun'r, on the north with the town common & on the south with the street or highway. *Signed:* Daniel Rumboll; Sarah Rumboll [mark]. *Date:* 13 October 1675. *Release of dower:* Sarah Rumboll, wife. *Witnesses:* Samuell Smith; Edw. Norrice, sen'r. *Acknowledged:* 1:9mo:75. *Recorded:* 30:2mo:1679.

THOMAS SKINNER & ELIZABETH SKINNER to JOHN TURNER – (5:143) Thomas Skinner (baker) and wife, Elizabeth, of Boston sold to John Turner (merchant) of Salem for consideration of 140 pounds the messuage or tenement with all land belonging to same, upland & meddow, 1½ acre in Salem bounded on the east by land of Richard Flinder, on the north by land of William West, & on the west by land of the said John Turner, & on the south by the sea or harbour, together with all houses, warehouses, edifices, buildings, fences... *Signed:* Thomas Skinner; Elizabeth Skinner. *Release of Dower:* Elizabeth Skinner. *Witnesses:* John Waite; John Hayward, sr. *Acknowledged:* 1 May 1679 by both. *Recorded:* 7 May 79.

THOMAS SKINNER to JOHN TURNER – (5:146) Thomas Skinner (baker) of Boston sold to John Turner (merchant) of Salem for sum of 200 & 80 pounds & bound himself for payment, the condition is such that if John Turner shall have & enjoy all messuage or tenement in Salem containing one acre and a half, bounded on the east side by the land of Richard Flinder, on the north by land of William West, on the west by land of the said John Turner, & on the south by the sea or harbour, according to deed bearing date with these presents without disturbance of Tho. Skinner & Elizabeth, wife, then this obligation void. *Signed:* Thomas Skinner. *Date:* 1 May 1679. *Witnesses:* John Waite; John Hayward, Sr. *Acknowledged:* 1 May 1679. *Recorded:* 7 May 1679.

JOHN GROVER, Sr. to ANTHONY WOOD – (5:148) John Grover Sr. (husbandman) of Beverly sold to Anthony Wood [called Thomas Wood in one place] (mariner) of Beverly for consideration of 3 pounds 10 shillings, land in Beverly consisting of one half acre of upland, bounded southerly with land of Edmund Grover, westerly with the highway or common road, northerly with the land of John Bennett, & easterly the land of the aforesaid Edmond Grover, with all right he had or would have by decease of father & covenanted that he owned land at decease of father, Edmond Grover.

Signed: John Grover. *Date:* 22 September 1673. *Witnesses:* Isaake Woodbery; Andrew Elliot. *Acknowledged:* 11:12:79 by John Grover & acknowledged by Edmund Grover [no date]. *Recorded:* 7:3:1679.

JAMES GRINDALL to PHILLIP BRIMBLECOM – (5:149) James Grindall of Old England bound himself to Phillip Brimblecom for 4 years apprentice beginning 3rd day of June next ensuing during which time sd apprentice shall serve & precepts & commandments lawfully doe in everye respect: as for any unlawful games, ye sd apprentice shall not play as cards, dice or any unlawfull games, whereby his said master may come to receive any hurt. As for marriage, he may not contract with any one during the time of the apprenticeship, but in all things behave himselfe faithfull & true as a servant ought to be: & sd master promised & covenanted to & with the ye sd apprentice to give hin sufficient meat, drink, aparell, washing & lodging & to keepe him in sicknes as well as in health, the time of his apprenticeship & at the expiration of the term of 4 whole yeares being fully compleat & ended, the sd master shall give to apprentice three pounds in silver, & two sutes of apparrell, one good & decent for Sabath daies & ye other for working daies. *Signed:* James Grindall [mark]. *Date:* 12 May 1679. *Witnesses:* Daniel King; Edward Humphryes. *Acknowledged:* 12:3mo:79. *Recorded:* 13 May: 79.

ZACHEUS GOULD to DANIEL CLEARK & THOMAS BAKER – (5:151) Zacheus Gould of Topsfield sold to Daniel Cleark of Topsfield & Thomas Baker for consideration of 34 pounds paid by Bates, one parcel of upland in Topsfield containing fourteen acres bounded with a brook toward the south, a highway toward the east & the land of Luke Wakelin towards the north & land of Barzila Barker towards the west. And one parcel of meadow containing six acres in Topsfield in the village, bounded with land of Zacheus Gould toward the south & Tho. Perkins land toward the north, by the meadow of Robert Smith towards the west & the meadow of Luke Wakeline towards the east. Daniel Cleark must maintain a fence on the south side of the aforementioned premises so far as they lie against the land of Zacheus Gould & Thomas Perkins. *Signed:* Zacheus Gould; Tho. Baker. *Date:* 17 January 1664. *Witnesses:* John Gould; Thomas Gidding. *Acknowledged:* 28 March 1665. *Recorded:* 15 May: 79.

WILLIAM DODGE to WILLIAM HASKALL – (5:152) William Dodge (husbandman) of Beverly sold to William Haskall (seaman) for consideration of 9 pounds, 10 acres of upland in Beverly bounded easterly with a meadow of Nehemiah Grover, south with land of Henry Herrick, north with land of Roger Conant & John Woodberry, & westerly land of William Dodge, sen'r. *Signed:* William Dodge. *Date:* 12 May 1679.

Witnesses: Thomas Robbins; Edm. Humphryes. *Acknowledged:* 12:3mo:79. *Recorded:* 15 May: 79.

DAVID PHIPPEN to ROBERT HODGE, NEHEMIAH WILLOUGHBY, ELEAZER GEDNEY, & FRANCES SKERRY – (5:154) David Phippen (shipwright) of Salem sold to Robert Hodge (mariner), Nehemiah Willoughby (merchant), Eleazer Gedney (shipwright) & Frances Skerry (yeoman), all of Salem, for consideration of 125 pounds sterling, the hull of a new ketch lately built & launched by the said David Phippen & finished & fitted for the sea with all carpenter work, boat & masts & yards to the said catch belonging, the said catch being named & called by the name of Frances & Mary of Salem, and of burthen thirty one ton or thereabouts, now lying or riding at anchor in the south river belonging to Salem, by the wharf of the said David Phippen to each their quarter part. *Signed:* David Phippen. *Date:* 17 May 1679. *Witnesses:* Nathaniel Pickman, sen'r; Hilliard Veren, sen'r. *Acknowledged:* 17:3mo:1679. *Recorded:* 15:3mo:1679.

EDMOND BATTER to STEPHEN SMALE – (5:156) Edmond Batter of Salem sold to Stephen Smale of Salem for consideration of 5 pounds, two acres of upland in the north field near the great cove, bounded on the north side by Nathaniel Felton's land, on the south of that land which formerly was the ten acre lot of the said Batter's, being part of that lot. Sd 2 acres being formerly in possession of John Robinson, deceased. *Signed:* Edmund Batter. *Date:* 19 May 1679. *Witnesses:* Stephen Small; Henry Skerry, sen'r. *Acknowledged:* 19:3mo:79. *Recorded:* 19:3mo:1679.

JAMES RUSSELL & ROBERT KNIGHT - (5:157) Whereas the town of Gloucester in 11th month of 1643 granted Richard Blindman, formerly minister of Gloucester, a certain farm or parcel of land at or near a certain cove, commonly called Ketle cove, containing four score acres of upland & all the neck of land beyond the marsh there, with a certain parcel of marsh there, being butted & bounded as by the records of the said town of Gloucester & whereas sd Richard Blindman many years since sold unto Richard Russell late of Charlestown, Esq. now deceased & whereas Richard Russell 8 of 4th month 1659 did convey same to Robert Knight of Marblehead, James Russell, son of sd Richard Russell for confirmation & for valuable sum of money pt paid Richard Russell in his lifetime and pt paid James Russell by Robert Knight, granted...& sold Robert Knight all farm, neck of land & marsh. *Signed:* James Russell. *Date:* 21 May 1679. *Witnesses:* Joseph Shapley; Eleazer Moody, sen'r; John Hayward, sen'r. *Acknowledged:* 21:May:1679. *Recorded:* 22:May:79.

RICHARD HAINES & MARY HAINES to JOHN SAMPSON – (5:161) Richard Haines of Beverly & wife Mary in consideraton they were ancient & desired to be freed of incumbrances of worldly business being past bodily labor, gave son-in-law John Sampson the full and free possession in fee simple of their personal estates, housing, lands & out housing & whatsoever shall appertain to be proper state to either & each of them only of cattle they reserved a four or five year old steer to the use of Nathaniel Carrill, disposed of when they see cause to give it to him. Also, if they died within three or four years, then four pounds out of their estate should be paid to Mary the wife of Nathaniel Carrill, after their decease. Also, Nathaniell Pease to have a two-year old heifer after their decease, from the said John Sampson, provided that John Sampson maintained Richard Haines and his wife, Mary during the rest of their natural lives...living by themselves during such time as they desired were capable of soe doing, in failure whereof sd Richard Haines or Mary his wife, after his decease, should have power to reenter the estate only that they should pay againe to Sampson whatsoever should appear that he deposited in their proper maintenance... *Signed:* Richard Haines; Mary Haines [mark]; John Sampson. *Date:* 14 September 1677. *Witnesses:* John Gally; Samuell Hardie. *Acknowledged:* by both 27 November 1677. *Recorded:* 22:May:1679.

RICHARD HAYNES to JOHN SAMPSON – (5:163) Richard Haynes (husbandman) of Beverly sold to John Sampson (husbandman) of Beverly for valuable consideration to be paid at time appointed, four acres & a half & eight rods of land in Beverly, bounded as follows: four acres having the land of the said Richard Haines on the south side & the broadway on the west, the land of Robert Hibbert on the north & Mr. Hale's land on the east, half acre adjoining on the east end to the cow lane & south side by Richard Haines' orchard & on the west end the land of Richard Haines & the north side to Mr. Hales' land, eight rods below the great rock adjoining to the cow lane. Land conveyed with a way through the said Richard Haines' land where it is most convenient to the said John Sampson. Land delivered by turf & twig in the presence of Thomas Picton & Gilbert Tapley, 29:of 10mo:71. *Signed:* Richard Haines; Mary Haines [mark]. *Date:* 29 December 1671. *Release of dower:* Mary Haines [mark]. *Witnesses:* Thomas Picton; Edward Bonds. *Acknowledged:* 22:9mo:1673. *Recorded:* 22:May:1679.

JOHN SAMPSON – (5:165) John Sampson (husbandman) of Beverly in consideration of 100 pounds in money & other goods received of brother-in-law John Pease (husbandman) of Salem deeded all & every part of his land, house & housing, goods & chattels, movables & immovables, with what other estates soever within doors & without known to belong to be his

in the town of Beverly, together with a piece of land consisting of about forty acres purchased of Nathaniell Felton in the township of Salem, provided if Sampson shall pay unto John Pease, the sum of one hundred pounds within two years from the day & date hereof then instrument to be voyd. *Signed:* John Sampson. *Date:* 23 May 1679. *Witnesses:* Richard Croade; Frances Croad [mark]. *Acknowledged:* 24:3mo:1679. *Recorded:* 24:May:79.

ELIZUR HOLYOKE to THOMAS BANCROFT – (5:167)   Elizur Holyoke (merchant) of Boston sold to Thomas Bancroft of Linn for a valuable consideration 1½ acre in Linn bounds, near Beaver Dam at the east corner of his farm lately sold [to] James Russell of Charlestown, bounded by the fences that are now about it...without contradiction of sd Elizur Holyoke or Mary Holyoke, wife. *Signed:* Elyzur Holyoke; Mary Holyoke. *Date:* 20 August 1678. *Witnesses:* Jacob Eliot; Mary Eliot. *Acknowledged:* March 7:78/9. *Recorded:* 7:June:79.

CHRISTOPHER LATTAMORE to JOHN PETHERICK – (5:169) Christopher Lattamore (vitner) of Marblehead sold to John Petherick (fisherman) of Marblehead neck for consideration of forty pounds sterling a parcel of land on Marblehead neck containing four acres being part of an eight acre lot formerly bought of John Goyte by his father, William Pitts, bound northerly by the highway that runs by the water side next to the great harbor, & some land of the said John Petherick lately bought of Mr. William Browne to the east, by the common land southerly, and a highway that runs cross the neck westerly. *Signed:* Christopher Lattamore [mark]. *Date:* 20 December 1678. *Witnesses:* Hannah Veren; Hilliard Veren, Sr. *Acknowledged:* 9:4mo:79. *Recorded:* 16:4mo:1679.

JOHN MECARTER to JEREMIAH MEACHAM – (5:171)   John Mecarter (dyer) of Salem sold to Jeremiah Meacham, his father-in-law, of Salem in consideration of 100 pounds in silver, his dwelling house, housing and shop which he built on land of his father-in-law between the house and land of Robert Wilson southerly, & the house and land of his father-in-law northerly. *Signed:* John Mecarter [mark]. *Date:* 9 June 1679. *Witnesses:* Sarah Ibrook; Richard Croade. *Acknowledged:* 10:4mo:79. *Recorded:* 20:4mo:1679.

THADDEUS RIDDAN to JOHN CHIN – (5:173) Thaddeus Riddan of Marblehead for consideration of a certain summe of money, sold to John Chin (cooper) of Marblehead one piece of ground lying and being in Marblehead, 31½ feet in the front, next to the street southwest; and northwest adjoining to the said Riddan's land; northeast adjoining to the

land of Nathaniell Walton's; and on the east side, adjoining with the land of Samuel Morgan's. In length it running down to the stone wall of Nathaniell Walton's land, it being at the lower end, 36 feet four inches in breadth as fenced in by said Chin & sd John Chin is to maintain fence. *Signed:* Thaddeus Riddan; Eliz: Riddan. *Release of dower:* Wife yielded dower. *Date:* 30 Julie 1677. *Witnesses:* Charles Green [mark]; Edm. Hunphreye. *Acknowledged:* 23:4mo:79. *Recorded:* 23:4mo:79.

JOHN HUDSON to RICHARD KNOTT – (5:176) John Hudson & Mary, wife, of Marblehead for a valuable consideration of a sum of money, sold to Richard Knott (cherurgeon) of Marblehead all his dwelling house and garden already fenced in, whereon the house now stands, situate, lying & being in Marblehead aforesaid. *Signed:* Jon. Hudson [mark]; Mary Hudson [mark]. **Date:** 1 May 1674. **Witnesses:** Robert Bartlett; Bethiah Bartlett; Thos. Robinson. *Acknowledged:* 13:3mo:74. *Recorded:* 30:4mo:1679.
"There is an assignment of this deed entered in foll. 15: of this book."

THOMAS MAULE to JOSHUA BUFFUM – (5:178) Thomas Maule (shopkeeper) of Salem & Naomi, wife, for a valuable sum sold to Joshua Buffum (carpenter) of Salem one dwelling house in the township of Salem, together with an orchard and an acre of land, lying to it, together with the trees belonging to the same, bounded by land of Phillip Cromwell, east; upon the river, north; upon land of Thomas Coale, west; and on the land of old Gaskin, south. And also two acres and one half against the north river, south; on the land of the Widdow Spooner, east; against the rockes of old Bishop, north; and on the lands of the Widdow Buffum, west. All which was formerly in the hands of Samuell Belknap. *Signed:* Thomas Maule; Naomi Maule [mark]. *Date:* 30 January 1678. *Witnesses:* George Deane; Francis Neale. *Acknowledged:* 2:5thmo:79 by both. *Recorded:* 4 July 1679.

JOHN ALFORD to EDMOND BATTER – (5:181) John Alford (seaman) of Salem for consideration of 11 pounds, 5 shillings sold to Edmond Batter (merchant) of Salem his dwelling house he lived in with all the ground thereto belonging and adjoining thereto, containing thirty poles of ground in Salem bounded by the lane or street to the north; the house and ground of John Lambert, west; land of Mr. John Rucksmith and the house and ground of Edward Feveryeare to the east. If sd John Alford pay Edmond Batter 11 pounds 5sh. at two payments of 5 pounds, 12 shillings and 6 pence in good dry fish, merchantable or refuse at or before the first of October next ensuing & 5 pounds 12 sh. & 6 pence more at or before October 1680 then this sale to be voyd.. *Signed:* John Alford [mark].

Date: 20 April 1679. *Witnesses:* Hilliard Veren, sen'r; Stephen Sewall. *Acknowledged:* 2:5mo:79. *Recorded:* 4:5:1679.

ELIAS WHITE to RICHARD KNOTT – (5:184) Elias White (fisherman) of Marblehead for a considerable sum of money sold to Richard Knott of Marblehead all his right, title and interest in that house & land whereon ye house standeth, that joineth unto Henry Trevitts land. *Signed:* Elias White. *Date:* 17 February 1678/9. *Witnesses:* Robert Sweet; Robert Nicholls. *Acknowledged:* 13:2mo:78:9. *Recorded:* 4:5:79.

GEORGE MAGER to JOHN LEGROE – (5:185) George Mager formerly of Jersey now of Newbury, son of Phillip Mager Parish of St. Laurance in Island of Jersey, deceased, for consideration of 11 pounds granted to John Legroe (mariner) of St. Laurance, Island of Jersey & now in Salem & bound home for Jersey his right to interest in messuage tenement the house & land thereto belonging in parish of St. Laurance, Isle of Jersey, now in tenure of Richard Browne also whatever else estate & he had a right in in said Island of Jersey, & I have put sd John Legroe in full possession of all premises by apiece of money called six-pence fixed in seale hereof & for the better recovery of sd debts or messuage or tenement goods chattels or all & singular premises made sd John Legroe true & lawful attorney to ask sue levy.,, *Signed:* George Mager [mark]. *Date:* 18 July 1679. *Witnesses:* Manasses Marston; Hilliard Veren, Sr.; Adrion de Mareston testemoni; Jean Bertaute est le marque X. *Acknowledged:* 18 July 1679. *Recorded:* 19 July 1679.

THOMAS GATCHELL to THADDEUS RIDDAN – (5:189) Thomas Gatchell (tailor) of Marblehead for certain sum of money sold to Thaddeus Riddan of Marblehead land and house standing upon the rock neere Tho. Dod's house in Marblehead with lands thereto belonging with all land between the house & highway to the southeast & 8 feet toward the southwest, 4 feet from the back side of the house to the northwest & from the northeast end of the house as far as the rocks go towards the highway which sd rocks or land was granted to Tho. Gatchell by towne with one cowes earbidg. *Signed:* Thomas Gatchell. *Date:* 7 October 1678. *Witnesses:* William Buckley; Samuell Gatchell. *Acknowledged:* 23:4:79. *Recorded:* 22:5mo:1679.

SAMUEL FRAILE to HENRY ROADS, Sr. – (5:192) Samuel Fraile (wheelwright) of Essex County for consideration of 10 pounds sold to Henry Roads, Sr. of Linn four acres of meadow in Stone's meadow in Linn, bounded easterly by Stone's brook; westerly by land of Robert Bates; northerly with land of Henry Collins, Sr.; southerly by the land of Thomas

Bancroft. *Signed:* Samuel Fraile. *Date:* 21 January 1678/79. *Witnesses:* George Keason; Thomas Mould. *Acknowledged:* 21:11mo:78. *Recorded:* 22 July 1679. 19 May 1679 Samuel Fraile delivered by turf & twigg meddow contained within deed. *Signed:* Samuell Fraile. *Witness:* Robert Bates [mark].

THOMAS MOULD to HENRY ROADS – (5:194) Thomas Mould (carpenter) of Salem for consideration of 11 pounds, 10 shillings sold to Henry Roads of Linn two and a half acres of salt marsh in the first division, in Rumny Marsh, Linn, bounded on the east by land of George Keasor, Sr.; on the west with land of Thomas Mould; on the north with "Bread's ditch" so-called; on the south end buts upon the cove. *Signed:* Thomas Mould. *Date:* 8 April 1679. *Witnesses:* George Keyser; Elizer Keyser. *Acknowledged:* 25:4mo:79. *Recorded:* 22:5mo:1679. Mary Mould did freely assent. *Signed:* Mary Mould.

GEORGE CORWIN to JOHN HILL – (5:196) George Corwin (merchant) of Salem for consideration of 12 pounds sold to John Hill (wheelwright) of Salem three quarters of an acre of meadow in Salem above the Traske mill in the North River, bounded southerly and easterly with land of Samuel Gardner, sen'r and northerly and westerly by the river. *Signed:* George Corwin; Elizabeth Corwin. *Release of dower:* Elizabeth Corwin. *Date:* 22 July 1679. *Witnesses:* John Whiting, Jr.; Hilliard Veren, clerk. *Acknowledged:* 23:5mo:79 by both. *Recorded:* 23:3mo:79.

JERARD SPENCER to Capt. GEORGE CORWIN – (5:198) Jerard Spencer of Haddam, CT for diverse good causes & considerations quitclaimed to Capt. George Corwin of Salem right to two parcels of land in Salem containing twenty-five acres. Twenty acres within fence and is within a greater parcel of forty acres and is bounded by the great pond on the east; the rockes on the northwest; Linn bounds on the southwest; a swamp on the northeast; & five acres on the west side of the pond. *Signed:* Gerard Spencer. *Date:* 15 May 1679. *Witnesses:* John Allen; George Gardner. *Acknowledged:* May 15, 1679 by Ensign Jerard Spencer at Hartford. *Recorded:* 25:5mo:1679.

EDWARD NORRICE to EDMOND BATTER - (5:200) Edward Norrice of Salem, schoolmaster, for 7 pounds, sold to Edmond Batter ¼ acre Salem, part of land that belonged to his dwelling house, behind the house to west and bounded by his land easterly, land of said Edmond Batter southerly and some land he lately sold to George Boothe westerly and land of Ezekiell Cheevers northerly and he warranted against all claims of son Edward

Norrise. *Signed:* Edw. Norrice, Sr. *Date:* 20 August 1679. *Witnesses:* Nathaniell Wallis; Hilliard Veren, Sr. recorder. *Recorded:* 26:6:1679.

ELLIAS STILEMAN to EDWARD WHARTON - (5:202) Ellias Stileman of Pascattaque river, for a parcell of glass, sold to Edward Wharton of Salem, glasier, a small piece of land next adjoining said Edward Wharton's dwelling house in Salem on the back side thereof in breadth from house at northern corner by now fence of Stileman's yard 21 foot and then to the northern of Capt. George Corwin's garden fence behind his warehouse, Wharton to keep all fence against land of Stileman so far as the premisses extend at Wharton's own cost. *Signed:* Elias Stileman. *Date:* 31 August 1668. *Witnesses:* Samuell Shattuck; John Robinson and premises given by turf and twig. *Acknowledged:* 23:6mo:79. *Recorded:* 26:6:79.

GEORGE CLEEVES to JOHN LEWES - (5:204) George Cleeves of Casco, gentleman, for 5 pounds stirling and yearly rent of 2 shillings and 2 days work for one man at any time when said work shall be called for all service and demand, rent to be paid every year at or upon first of November and paid to him or assigns forever, sold to John Lewes, eldest son of George Lewes of Casco, 100 acres of land, together in Casco Bay bordering upon the bounds of John's father's former grant of 50 acres and westerly from John's house on same side of water and beginning his westerly bounds, at third creek from said George Lewis' house westerly and by water side easterly so many pole to bounds of John's father's former grant and upon that bredeth to woods from the water side northwest and by west till the hundred acres be ended and so much marsh as is growing as belonging to every hundred acres of upland in his whole grant. *Signed:* George Cleeves. *Date:* 26 June 1657. *Witnesses:* Richard Waters; George Ingersoll; John Swinerton. *Acknowledged:* 2 April 1661. *Recorded:* 13:7mo:1679.

JOHN LEWIS & ELLENOR LEWIS to NATHANIELL WALLIS, SR. - (5:205) John Lewis and Ellenor wife for 18 pounds sold to Nathaniell Wallis, Sr. all their right title and interest of premises and also 3 acres of marsh in great marsh above the plantation not mentioned in the deed. *Signed:* John Lewis [mark]; Elnor Lewis [mark]. *Date:* 27 February 1674. *Witnesses:* Robert Corbin; Nathaniel Wallis. *Acknowledged:* 27:12mo:74 (by both). *Recorded:* 13:7mo:79.

NATHANIELL WALLIS, Sr. to EDMOND GALE - (5:206) Nathaniell Wallis, Sr. with consent of wife Margirett late inhabitant of Casco, now resident in Beverly for valuable sum sold to Edmond Gale of Beverly, fisherman, all right to bill of sale or deed written on the other side of paper and also the assignment on back side of deed of land assigned to him by

John Lewis and wife Ellenor with all land, marsh and other privileges mentioned in deed or assignment. *Signed:* Nathaniell Wallis; Margarett Wallis [mark]. *Date:* 10 February 1678/9. *Witnesses:* Frances Neale, Sr.; Frances Neal, Jr. *Acknowledged:* by both with no date. *Recorded:* 13:7:79.

JOHN LEWIS to NATHANIELL WALLIS, Sr. - (5:207) John Lewis of Falmouth, alias Casco, County of York, (with consent of wife Ellenor) planter, for 18 pounds in money and goods at money price sold to Nathaniell Wallis, Sr. of Falmouth, all plantation where he lived in Falmouth, alias Casco, being 100 acres of upland as mentioned in deed he received from Mr. George Cleeves dated 26 June 1657 wherein rent was mentioned and 3 acres of marsh in Falmouth, alias Casco, at great marsh. *Signed:* John Lewis [mark]; Elenor Lewis [mark]. *Date:* 20 March 1674. *Witnesses:* John Wakely; Bartho: Wallis; George Joanes [mark]. *Recorded:* 13:7:1679.

NATHANIELL WALLIS, Sr. to EDMOND GALE - (5:209) Nathaniell Wallis, Sr. late of Casco Bay, inhabitant, now resident in Beverly, having bought land and marsh of John Lewis late of Casco which John Lewis bought of Mr. George Cleeves 26 June 1657, which he already assigned over to Edmond Gale of Beverly, fisherman, with consent of wife Margarett assigned over all right to deed of marsh and all therein contained. *Signed:* Nathaniell Wallis; Marggrett Wallis [mark]. *Date:* 13 February 1678. *Witnesses:* Frances Neal, Sr.; Frances Neale, Jr. *Acknowledged:* 13:12:78 by both.

SAM'LL VERRY to WILLIAM TRASK & JOHN TRASK - (5:210) Sam'll Verry of Salem, husbandman, with consent of wife for 10 pounds sold to William Trask and John Trask of Salem 5 acres of land on the neck in Salem between house of John Sothwick and house of said Sam'll Verry bounded on northerne side by land of said Wm and John Trask, on wersterne side by land of said John Sothwick and on sotherne side by land of said Samuell Verry, being 20 pole wide at westerne end and runs taper coming to point at easterne end and adjoining to land of said Wm and John Trask on northerne side and bounds both westward and eastward upon John Sothwick's lands. *Signed:* Samuell Verry. *Date:* 2 April 1678. *Witnesses:* Humphry Case; Anthony Needham. *Acknowledged:* 16:11mo: 78. *Recorded:* 15:7:79.

WILLIAM TRASK to JOHN TRASK - (5:212) William Trask of Salem, yeoman, for good causes, especially natural affection to brother John Trask of Salem and for settling estate left by father Wm Trask deceased, deeded to

John Trask, his brother, of Salem, several parcells of land: half an acre of salt marsh in Salem toward north river head above mills, bounded on east with some land of Elizabeth Spooners on north with some land of John Loomes and south and west by river; also half acre more of salt marsh upon same river bounded on east by land of John Sanders, north by upland of said John Trask, west by land of said Wm Trask, south by river; also ½ of all interest of all land called old mill pond; also half acre of salt marsh on a point on said river in north side of orchard belonging to their dwelling house, on south side of river, also half of parcel of marsh by Daniell Sothwick's bounded by land of said Daniell Sothwick southeast and river northwest. *Signed:* Wm. Trask. *Date:* 2 April 1678. *Witnesses:* Humpry Case; Samuell Verye. *Acknowledged:* 16:8mo:78. *Recorded:* 15:7:78 [between deeds recorded 79].

WILLIAM TRASK to JOHN TRASK - (5:214) William Trask of Salem, miller, for 20 pounds sold to John Trask, his brother, of Salem his part of dwelling house that John possessed which was willed by their father's legacy between them and also his part of house and garden and the northerne end of said house, together with a piece of salt marsh on northerne side of river almost over against said house, ¼ acre bounded on northwest side by Anthony Needham's meddow, easterly upon John's own meddow, north upon John's own upland and south upon the river. *Signed:* William Trask. *Date:* 2 April 1678. *Witness:* Humpry Case. *Acknowledged:* 16:11mo:78. *Recorded:* 15:7:79.

EDWARD RICHARDS to DANIELL RICHARDS - (5:216) Edward Richards of Linn (with consent of Ann his wife) for divers good causes and more especially for entire love and parental afection for beloved son Daniell Richards deeded to Daniell Richards the moyetie or ½ part of his dwelling house at northeast end of town of Linn and ½ of all land belonging to said dwelling house or near adjoining, 25 acres of land, bounded by town comon on northwest and ranging along by land of Benjamin Farr on northeast and southeast and land of Ezekiell Needham on southeast and also ½ of gardens, orchards, timber, fruit trees and housing, fencing, mines, minerals and comonage. *Signed:* Edward Richards [mark]; Ann Richards. *Date:* 8 December 1679. *Witnesses:* John Davis; Jacob Knight. *Acknowledged:* 10:7mo:79 by Edward and Daniell Richards. *Recorded:* 15:7:79.

SAMUEL EBORNE to JOHN ROBINSON - (5:219) Samuel Eborne of Salem, husbandman, for valuable sum sold to John Robinson of Topsfield, husbandman, 1 acre 20 pole upland said acre being formerly a grant to Zacheus Curtice by towne of Salem and the 20 pole bought by said Curtice of Joshua Veren there being an old cellar digged in said 20 rod, said 1 acre and 20 rod lying near farm formerly Mr. Batter's and Mr. Johnson's farms and bounded with or near brook called Brooksby on west northerly comon land to the southward and northerly with parcel of land of Hilliard Veren's also 1 parcel more being all meadow above Mr. Clark's meadow formerly now Mr. Gedney's on the southwesterly and on north with Dogg Pond Plain and Mr. Humphry's farm or near southeasterly said parcel of meddow or low land being given to Zacheus Curtice formerly by Town of Salem and by him sold to John Robinson and by him sold to Sam'l Eborne, and by him now sold to said Robinson, 20 acres. *Signed:* Samuell Aborne. *Date:* 5 June 1679. *Witnesses:* Henry West; Hilliard Veren, Sr. *Acknowledged:* 23: 5mo:79 & wife, Susanna, yielded right. *Recorded:* 13:8:79.

HENRY BARTHOLMEW to JOHN ROBINSON - (5:221) Henry Bartholmew of Salem sold to John Robinson of Salem a parcell of meddow ground 3 acres which was sometime in possession of Thomas Scudden of Salem northward of Ipswich river bounded with land of Thomas and Nathaniell Putnam on southwest and with comon land on northwest and butting toward river southward having some comon land between it and the river. *Signed:* Henry Bartholmew. *Date:* 5th of 5th mo. 1669. *Witnesses:* Nathaniell Beadle; Israell Porter. *Acknowledged:* 22:5mo.:79. *Recorded:* 13:8:1679.

JACOB GREENE & MARY GREENE to DANIELL HICHINS - (5:222) Jacob Greene and Mary, wife, of Charlestown for 220 pounds sold to Daniell Hichins of Linn his farm, being a tract of upland and meddow or marsh ground there unto belonging with the messuage, tenement and farmhouse and other buildings on part standing, now in tenure and occupation of said Hichins, formerly the estate and in tenure and occupation of Samuell Bennett of Rumney marsh, bounded on west westwardly by lands of Capt. Thomas Brattle, on north with hills bounding that part called Plow plaine at north and north easterly side bounded by high ledge of rockes and runing down to pond; on easterly end bounded partly by pond and partly by brooke runing into pond over against which said runing brooke stands before mentioned house and buildings together also with upland of 6 acres on easterly side of said brooke; also moyety or equall half part of Squire's meddow within Maulden bounds; also 14 acres of salt marsh in Rumney marsh formerly purchased of Capt. Robert Bridges, formerly called the 14-acre lott bounded on easterly side of a salt creek with land of Thomas Newell southeast, land of Samuell Johnson northeast and with lands of John Ballard southwest. *Signed in Boston:* Jacob Greene; Mary Greene; Wm. Bartholmew consented and signed. *Date:* 24 September 1679. *Witnesses:* Wm. Kilcupp; George Briggs.

EBENEZER GARDNER & SAMUELL GARDNER - (5:226) Ebenezer Gardner being by last will and testament of father George Gardner, lately deceased, together with his brother Samuell Gardner made executors constituted his well beloved brother Samuell Gardner of Salem to be lawfull aturney to ask, sue for, levy, require, recover and receive of all and every person such debts, rents and sums of money due to him or by said will of father due to him or any legatee therein mentioned at any day or time that shall be due, owing, belonging or appertaining unto by any manner of means and granted attorney authority in premises and upon receipt of any such debts, rents and sumes of money or discharges to make and deliver all and every act and acts, things and things, device and devices in law necessary to be done in or about premises for recovery of any such debts or for paying any legacies or debts due. *Signed:* Ebenezer Gardner. *Date:* 25 October 1679. *Witnesses:*   John Hathorne, John Higginson, Jr. *Acknowledged:* no date. *Recorded:* 27:8:1679.

JOHN MASSEY to JEREMIAH NEAL & PETER CHEEVER - (5:227) John Massey of Salem, husbandman, for a valuable sum of money sold to Jeremiah Neale, carpenter, and Peter Cheever, glover, both of Salem a small tract of land and marsh, 9 acres of upland and half acre salt marsh lying together in north field in Salem, bounded: the half acre lying on west of said upland bounded on west by a creeke and on north and south with meddow and upland of Jeremiah Neale, the whole quantity of upland bounded on west with 2 parcels of marsh belonging to Jeremiah Neale and the half acre in the middest and the upland is bounded on south with land which was formerly John Neales, in possession of Jonathan Neale on east, with land of Henry Skerry, Jr. and and other lott of said Massey's, on north with land of Frances Skerry and if above land should not be fully 9 acres, then John Massey to make it up out of his other lott of land caled Shippis lott, on east side of tract and to be laid out next adjoining to land. *Signed:* John Massey. *Date:* 3 June 1679. *Witnesses:* Frances Neale, Sr.; Frances Neale, Jr.   *Acknowledged:*   26:4mo.:79 and wife yielded interest. *Recorded:* 29:8:1679.

RICHARD HUCHENSON to THOMAS HALE, Jr. - (5:231) Richard Huchenson of Salem for several considerations and love and affection unto his daughter, Mary, wife of Thomas Hale, Jr. sold to Thomas Hale, Jr. of Newbury 20 acres of upland adjoining to land of Thomas Putnam, Sr. easterly and having the land of Thomas Putnam, Sr. northerly and land of Joseph Huchenson or the executors of John Huchenson deceased southerly:

said 20 acres being part of a parcell of land in possession of Richard Huchenson, about 200 acres, purchased of Major Wm. Hathorne and granted to him by town of Salem, the 20 acres being on easterly side of the hundred acres adjoyning land of Thomas Putnam, Sr. of Salem near his dwelling house and said 20 acres to run length of Richard's land being near a mile in length and of an equal bredth from end to end and to join all along land of Thomas Putnam, Sr. *Signed:* Richard Huchinson [mark]. *Date:* 30 October 1678. *Witnesses:* Nathaniel Putnam; Thomas Ferman; and land delivered by turf and Twig 19 September 1679. *Witnesses:* Nathaniell Putnam; Elizabeth Putnam [mark]. *Recorded:* 29:8:1679.

HENRY SEWALL & STEPHEN SEWALL - (5:233) Henry Sewall of Newbery formerly of North Badsley England for divers good causes and consideration constituted loving son Stephen Sewall, bound for England, to be lawfull atorney, for him and in his name to ask, demand, collect, take, recover and receive all and singular such sum and sums of money, debts, duties, rents, effects and things which were or that any day or time shall grow due, be owing, or payable to him, from all and every person or persons within realm of England by any waies or meanes, nothing excepted or reserved, with all costs, damages and interests. *Signed:* Henry Sewall. *Date:* 11 November 1679. *Witnesses:* Wm. Longfellow; Jacob Toppan; Nicholas Wallingford [mark]; Thomas Woodbridg; Wm. Noyce. *Acknowledged:* 11:9mo:1679. *Recorded:* 15:9mo:1679.

HENRY SEWALL & JANE SEWALL to STEEPHEN SEWALL - (5:235) Henry Sewall and Jane wife of Newbery formerly of North Badsly England, gentleman, for divers good causes especially for naturall good will, love and affection unto Steephen Sewall, their youngest son, deeded all messuage or tenement and land, medow, orchard and garden which Henry Sewall formerly purchased of John Good in Horton in the parrish of Bishopstoake county of South Hampton England that was or late in tenure or occupation of Mr. Steeven Dumer or assigns, together with all out houses stable barns edifices buildings woods underwoods trees and fences standing upon said lands or any part thereof...with all rents, issues and profits arising thereupon or from thence to be had, made or raised. *Signed:* Henry Sewall; Jane Sewall. *Date:* 11 November 1679. *Witnesses:* Wm. Longfellow; Jacob Toppan; Nicholas Woolingford [mark]; Tho. Woodbridge; Wm. Noyce. *Acknowledged:* November 11, 1679 by both. *Recorded:* 15:9mo:79.

RICHARD BRAYBROOK to JOHN POLIN - (5:238) Richard Braybrook of Wenham for 15 pounds sold to John Polin of Ipswich 6 acres of meadow in Wenham purchased of Thomas White of Wenham which was formerly granted to John White father to said Thomas White of Wenham as appeereth by Salem grant at town meeting 15th of 12th mo 1642 bounded southeast by lands or meadow of Richard Dodg the comon upon east and upon north and northeast by lands of Thomas Patch and upon south and southwest by comon land of Wenham. *Signed:* Richard Braybrook. *Date:* 2 February 1674. *Witnesses:* Richard Hubbard; Sarah Hubbard. *Acknowledged:* 30 January 1678. *Recorded:* 17:9mo:79.

ROBERT GRAY & ROBERT GRAY & Capt. NICHOLAS MANNING - (5:239) Robert Gray of Salem deceased in last will and testament bequeathed as a legacy to son Robert Gray a kitchin standing near his dwelling house with so much ground to be laid out to it as his overseers should in discretion see meete and accordingly the overseers of his will laid out to said Robert Graye and delivered to him his proper right to possess and enjoy forever 34 rod or pole of land bounded by a stake at front about 8 foot northward of the well and then to a post standing at bound of Samuell Beadle's land fronting to lane or comon highway and to run westward to end of said Beadle's fence which is near 10 rods and southward to a stake about 3½ rods from Samuell Beadle's fence and to run upon straite line to a stake near highway and whereas Capt. Nicholas Manning who married the relict widow and executrix removed said kitchen and in or near said place built a shop, the overseers determined that the shop shall be the estate of Robert Gray and being not of like value to the kitchin judged and determined that said Manning pay Gray 5 pounds. *Signed:* Henry Bartholmew; John Browne. *Date:* 28 9th mo 1679. *Acknowledged:* Mr. Henry Bartholomew and Mr. John Browne came into Court at Salem 28:9mo:1679. *Recorded:* 1:10mo:1679.

ANN COLE to JONATHAN CORWIN - (5:241) Ann Cole of Salem, relict and administratrix of estate of husband Thomas Cole for 45 pounds sold to Mr. Jonathan Corwin of Salem, merchant, 10 acre lott which had been in tenure and possession of deceased husband Thomas Cole in northfield in Salem bounded on land of said Mr. Jonathan Corwin easterly, westerly on land of Mr. Eleazer Gedney beginning from marked oak tree standing without fence on south end towards river and bounded straitly ranging along by said Gedney's land northwesterly and butts northerly upon a highway neer to land of Frances Skerry partly and partly on land of Ebenezer Gardner, southerly partly on salt marsh of James Symonds and then to marked oak tree to river. *Signed:* Ann Cole [mark]. *Date:* 22 October 1679. *Witnesses:* John Caley, Sr.; Richard Croad; Abraham Cole. *Acknowledged:* 21:9mo.:1679. *Recorded:* 1:10mo.: 1679.

JONATHAN BILES to RICHARD OBER - (5:244) Jonathan Biles of Beverly, carpenter, (Elizabeth wife yielded dower) for a valuable sum sold to Richard Ober of Beverly, seaman, 8 acres of upland in Beverly bounded easterly and southerly with comon land belonging to Beverly, westerly with land of Charles Kemball and northerly with land of Joseph Eaton and land of Joseph Dodg. *Signed:* Jonathan Biles; Eliza Biles [mark]. *Date:* 6th March 1678/9. *Witnesses:* Marke Tricker [mark]; John Patch. *Acknowledged:* 27:9mo.:79 by both. *Recorded:* 2:10mo.:1679.

JOSEPH GRAY to NICHOLAS MANNING - (5:246) Joseph Gray of Salem, gunsmith, for 15 pounds sold to his father in law Mr. Nicholas Manning of Salem ¼ acre in Salem being part of orchard adjoining and belonging to dwelling house of said Nicholas Manning bounded on north with land of John Priest, which was formerly given to "his" wife Elizabeth by her father deceased, on south with lands of said Nicholas Manning, westward with land of Mr. John Gedney, Sr. and eastward with street or highway: this being some land given by his father Robert Gray deceased. *Signed:* Joseph Gray. *Date:* 8 July 1673. *Witnesses:* Samuell Beadle; Edward Norrice, Sr.. *Acknowledged:* 5:8mo.:74. *Recorded:* 24:10:79.

CRISTOPHER CODNER to RICHARD KNOTT - (5:248) Cristopher Codner of Marblehead, seaman, for sum of money sold to Richard Knott of Marblehead, cherurgeon, ½ acre of land in Marblehead bounded on eastern end on John Northy's land, to south on land of William Nick and John Martin and to north and to west on land of said Richard Knott. *Signed:* Christopher Codner. *Date:* second day of September 1679. *Witnesses:* John Devorix; Humphry Devorix. *Acknowledged:* 29:7mo.:79. *Recorded:* 24:10mo.:79.

REUBEN GUPPY to WILLIAM GODSOE - (5:249) Reuben Guppy of Salem for valuable sum sold to William Godsoe of Salem 4 pole or rod of ground granted by town of Salem according to town grant and laid out betweene William Lord's house and the water side. *Signed:* Reuben Guppy [mark]; Elenor Guppy [mark]. *Date:* fourteenth of December 1678. *Witnesses:* John Guppy; Abigail Guppy [mark]; James Bukham; Thomas Ellyott. *Acknowledged:* 17:12mo.:78. *Recorded:* 24:10mo.:79.

RALPH KING & BLANO & RIDDAN & DANIELL KING - (5:251) 1st upon the acknowledgment of a deed 27 of 8th month 1670, it was agreed between Mr. King senior and his son Ralph that his 3 sons in law Blano and Riddan and his own son Daniell shall have free liberty to bring down their wood to the comon landing place. 2nd that Mr. King reserved to himself land which was Thomas Smith's on the hill within the field. 3rd that what the line in deed of gift shall take of from the old field given to Daniell, that what Ralph shall have of same that he shall make his brother satisfaction for the same as two indifferent men shall judge. 4th what engagement Mr. Blano hath at Boston, he hath free liberty to have wood of the farm, Ralph cutting it and he carting it and at water side to divide the same between them, this to be done between this and last Aprill next. *Signed:* Ralph King. *Witnesses:* William Hathorne, Sr.; John Collins. *Recorded:* 19:9mo.:70.

HILLIARD VEREN, Sr. & HILLIARD VEREN, Jr. - (5:251) Hilliard Veren, Sr of Salem for 30 pounds sold to Hilliard Veren, Jr of Salem ¼ acre of land in Salem bounded easterly with land of Thomas Putnam and on westerly side with land of Phillip Cromwell and at the south end by street and northerly by north river or way by north river side. *Signed:* Hilliard Veren, Sr.. *Date:* 29 November 1679. *Witnesses:* Bartho Gedney; John Higgenson, Jr. *Recorded:* 24:10:79.

THOMAS TRAPP & JOSHUA ATWATER - (5:253) Bill binding Thomas Trapp of Martin's Vineyard to pay Joshua Atwater of Boston 129 pounds 16 shillings and 3 pence for goods received. *Signed:* Thomas Trapp. *Date:* 30th day of 7ber 1675. *Witnesses:* Jonathan Jackson; Joshua Atwater, Jr. *Acknowledged:* 10 March 1679/80. *Recorded:* 9 July 1680.

HILLIARD VEREN, Jr. & HILLIARD VEREN, Sr. - (5:253) Hilliard Veren, Jr. of Salem, merchant, for 15 pounds sold to Hilliard Veren, Sr. of Salem 30 rods or pole of ground and part of ground belonging to his dwelling house in Salem lying with out the fence of his garden southerly and the lane that goes down to the south river bounds it westerly and the lane or highway that goes to Capt. Mores southerly and some land of Capt. William Brown's easterly and said garden fence northerly. *Signed:* Hilliard Veren, Jr. *Date:* 29 November 1679. *Witnesses:* Bartholomew Gedney; John Higgenson, Jr. *Recorded:* 24:10:79.

GEORGE MAY & ELIZABETH MAY to WILLIAM JAMISON - (5:255) Whereas Mathew Price of Salem sold to George Maye the house and land within mentioned and whereas there is a provision contained therein for redemption of the premises upon payment of 11 pounds upon 24th day of June 1673, which sum or any part thereof was not paid or rendered to be paid, said house and land with all other within mentioned premises became forfeited unto said George May, said George May and Elisabeth wife for 11 pounds sold the within mentioned said house and land to William Jamison of Charlestown, tailor. *Signed:* George May; Elizabeth May. *Date:* 15 August 1679. *Witnesses:* John Hayward, Sr.; Eleazer

Moody serv't. *Acknowledged:* 15 August 1679 by both. *Recorded:* 5:11:1679.

WILLIAM DIXY to RICHARD OBER - (5:257) William Dixy of Beverly for a valuable consideration sold to Richard Ober ½ acre land on east side of his own land near middle of Ober's fence and running northward to a bound tree standing in Richard Thissell's fence and also running southward to a marked tree to the sea side both which 2 later bounds marks near former land marks between said Ober and himself. *Signed:* William Dixy [mark]. *Date:* 20 December 1679. *Witnesses:* Nicholas Woodberry; Hugh Woodberry. *Acknowledged:* 7:11:79 by Capt. Wm. Dixy. *Recorded:* 7:11mo.:1679.

WILLIAM NICHOLLS to JOHN NICHOLLS & LIDEA NICHOLLS - (5:258) William Nicholls of Topsfield, husbandman, for divers good causes and especially for naturall love and affection to his son John Nicolls and wife Lidea sold them farm that he lived on in Topsfield of 150 acres bounded on east and so northerly with land of Benjamin Porter and southerly with land of Job Swinerton and Henry Keney and westerly with land of John Putnam and northerly with land that he gave to his adopted son Isaack Burton, during John's natural life and wife Lidea during her widowhood & after to their children, and reserved in his own hand all that part of field that he did now enjoy for his and wife's use and half the land unimproved to himself and wife during their natural life and then to John Nicholls and heirs forever. *Signed:* William Nicholls [mark]. *Date:* 6 January 1678. *Witnesses:* John Putnam, Sr.; Jonathan Putnam. *Acknowledged:* 15:11mo.:78. *Recorded:* 12:11mo:1679.

RESOLVED WHITE to ELIZABETH LORD - (5:260) Resolved White of Salem and Abigaile, wife and executrix of last will and testament of William Lord, deceased, for divers good causes and considerations and especially for love and natural affection to Elizabeth Lord, kinswoman to said William Lord deceased and the daughter of William Lord, Sr. now surviving and especially in order to fulfill last will and testament of said William Lord, deceased, deeded west end of dwelling house that John Bly now dwelt in standing by south river side in Salem containing 1 lower and 1 upper room, the lower room having a chimney in it, also ground said end of house stood on together with all ground to south side of whole house to water side with all right in the wharfe and all ground to water yielding and paying therefore yearly to said Resolved and Abigaile White or their assigns 40 shillings in money yearly during said Abigaile, executrix's natural life only, to be paid quarterly, 10 shillings every quarter. Memorandum that above yearly rent of 40 shillings is to be 35 shillings per annum; also that

Elizabeth shall have free liberty to make use of 3 foot in bredth of ground on back side of house to come from time to time to refrain said house or for other uses: the abatement of 5 shillings per annum is in consideration of refrain of the house: and liberty to come to well to draw water. *Signed:* Resolved White; Abigaile White [mark]. *Date:* 23 December 1679. *Witnesses:* Hilliard Veren, Sr.; Samuell Graye. *Acknowledged:* 12:11mo:79 by both. *Recorded:* 12: January: 79.

THOMAS VERRY to JEFFERY PARSONS - (5:263) Thomas Verry of Gloster, fisherman, (wife Hanah yielded dower) for 6 pounds stirling sold to Jeffery Parsons of Gloster, yeoman, 2 acres of land in Gloster in fishing field bounded westerly with comon land, northerly with land formerly of James Babsons now land of said Parsons, sotherly with land of John Collens and easterly with land formerly of Samuell Doliver now land of said Parsons. *Signed:* Thomas Verry [mark]; Hanah Verry [mark]. *Date:* 2 January 1679. *Witnesses:* Bethiah Rich [mark]; Hilliard Veren, Sr. *Acknowledged:* 2 January 1679. *Recorded:* 12:11mo:1679.

JOHN PRICE & ELIZABETH PRICE to PHILLIP ENGLISH - (5:266) John Price executor and Elizabeth Price, relict and executrix of will of Capt. Walter Price, deceased, for 56 pounds 10 shillings sold to Phillip English of Salem, marrenor, parcell of land said Walter Price deceased bought of John Steevens with dwelling house thereupon and a shop with a sellor under it, 30 or 40 rod in Salem as bounded and granted by the towne of Salem and late in occupation of Tobias Carter bounded sotherly with street, easterly with house and land that was late or is house and land of Jeremiah Booteman, northerly with comon land and westerly with land and house of said Phillip English. *Signed:* John Price; Eliza Price. *Date:* 22 day of December 1679. *Witnesses:* Mary Woolcot; John Croad. *Acknowledged:* 13:11:79 by Capt. Price and Mrs. Elizabeth Price. *Recorded:* 15:11:1679.

JOHANAH COLDUM & CLEMENT COLDUM - (5:268) Johanah Coldum, widow of Thomas Coldum, deceased, of Linn, in consideration that she was disabled by reason of age to manage her business and also being deprived of other half which her husband had left her, together with other good reasons moving her which were to be performed by son in law Clement Coldum of Gloster deeded him after her death other half of whole accomodation consisting of house, lands and orchard and meddow ground of all sorts in Linn which husband Thomas Coldum died in possession of, he having given said Clement Coldrum, his natural son ½ of whole accommodation of houses land and meddow ground of all sort in his last will, viz: after her death half the stock of cattle, to be in partnership between him and her undivided while she lived, viz: 2 oxen, 4 cows, 1 2-year calf, 1 mare, 2 young horses and 12 sheep together with cartes, plows, yoakes, chains and all tools and appurtenances for husbandry; that said Clement was to improve the whole living, both upland ground and other meddowes of all sorts well and profitably to their equal benefit viz: to deliver to her yearly in her house, half the produce of all the land in tillage by the bushel and of the orchard, the cider by the barrel and what was not made in cider the rest of fruit by measure and to find all the seed of the land at his own cost and at his own cost to keep all housing and fences in good repair and to pay all rates and to provide well for and carefully to look to all said stock of cattle of all sorts during her life and she was to have half the benefit thereof and he was to bring her to her house yearly during her life time convenient firewood and if need be bring it into her house and see to it carefully that she want not convenient attendance in time of sickness but be an assistant to her both in time of sickness and health during her life; and if they could not live comfortably together in her dwelling house, he was at her desire to build another by it for him to live in so that he could perform all the conditions and he was in 2 years time after her death to pay a good cow to daughter Mary Simonds or value of it and 5 pounds to Sarah Hart. *Signed:* Johanah Coldum [mark]; Clement Coldum. *Date:* 20 September 1675. *Witnesses:* Andrew Mansfield; Thomas Browne. *Acknowledged:* 23:2mo:1679. *Recorded:* 20:11mo:79.

EDWARD WILSON to BENJAMIN BROWNE - (5-271) Edward Wilson of Fairefield Coneticot, formerly of Salem, ship carpenter, for 9 pounds sold to Benjamin Browne of Salem, merchant, 1½ or 2 acres in Salem at or near poynt of rockes he was formerly possest of in his own right, being before land of Robert Codnam, bounded on easterly side by some land of Robert Follet's formerly of one John White, westerly by some land of Richard Hides, since by that land possest by Richard Hollingsworth and now by Phillip English, northerly by orchard and garden formerly of Richard Hollingsworth in part and partly by comon land, at northeast corner where premisses runs down to comon, crosse the end of Richard Hollingsworth's orchard and southerly by highway that goes by the water side. *Signed:* Edward Wilson [mark]. *Date:* 24 January 1679. *Witnesses:* Henry Higgenson; John Attwater. *Acknowledged:* 24:11mo:79. *Recorded:* 26:11mo:79.

BRIDGETT OLIVER to JOHN BLEVIN - (5:274) Bridgett Oliver, relict and administratrix of Thomas Oliver, late deceased, of Salem, for 45 pounds paid and secured to be paid with consent of Selectmen of Salem who subscribed and in order to satisfy and pay debts which estate of said Thomas Oliver stood indebted to several men, sold to John Blevin of Salem, yeoman, 10 or 11 acres her husband dyed possest of in north field in Salem bounded: by some land of James Symonds westerly the comon highway at northerly end and highway between premises and some land of Jeremiah Neales easterly and some marsh ground of said James Symonds by the water side southerly, said parcel called 10-acre lot. *Signed:* Bridgett Oliver [mark]. *Date:* 26 January 1679. *Witnesses:* Hilliard Veren, Sr.; Joseph Huchenson; Daniell Andrew. *Acknowledged:* 26:11:79. *Recorded:* 26:11mo:1679. Salem 26:11mo:79/80 The Selectmen of Salem consented to sale of said land according to an order of the County Court.

THOMAS CAVE to PEETER PRISCOTT - (5:276) Thomas Cave whose residence was near the outside bounds of Salem, near to outside bounds of Topsfield, planter, for 17 pounds sold to Peeter Priscott of Salem, planter, 17 acres in Salem, being part of a farm that was formerly Mr. John Ruck's, at south end of farm, bounded on south with dead tree bound of Capt. Lothrop and Thomas Putnam, land of Capt. Lothrop on east to heap of stones northward then with land of Phillip Knight on north end to white oak westerly then a little northerly by said Phillip's land on east to country road, then country highway and Thomas Cave's land on north to rock on south side of said road that is bound of Jonathan Knight, then with said Jonathan Knight's land on west to great red oak near meddow of John Hutchinson and stone at southeast side of tree near 4 foot over southeast of the rock that bounds then with said meddow on west and a little upland to dead tree of Capt. Lothrop and Thomas Putnam which is south bounds. *Signed:* Thomas Cave; Mary Cave. *Witnesses:* Nathaniel Veren; Thomas Putnam; Edward Putnam. *Acknowledged:* 20:of March:1677:8. *Recorded:* 27:11:79.

GEORGE CORWIN to JEREMIAH NEALE – (5:278) George Corwin (merchant) of Salem, with consent of wife, sold to Jeremiah Neale (carpenter) of Salem for a valuable consideration, two parcels of meddow ground scituate in ye northfeild of said towne, the one being a small of fresh medow ground, it being all the ground where he has right within the following bounds & being bounded as followeth. viz: eastward with a little brooke, southward with ye and of Mr. Bartholmew Gedney, & westward with ye highwaye on some lands formerly in ye possession of Mr. Hugh Peters or else ye towne comon; & the other being alsoe a small parcel of meddow ground containing about halfe an acre lying in sd Northfeild at a place caled Goodell's spring & having said spring within it & being compast on ye east with ye river that comes out of the broad cove on ye north with ye marsh ground formerly belonging to Mr. Hugh Peeters, but now in possession of Deacon Horne as also southerly & on ye southeast & southwest sides thereof with some upland likewise formerly belonging to said Mr. Hugh Peeters or else ye towne comon. *Signed:* George Corwin. *Date:* 25 February 1677:8. *Witnesses:* Edw. Norrice, senior; William Andrew. *Acknowledged:* 14:2mo:1679. *Recorded:* 29:11mo:1679.

WILLIAM LORD, senior to NICHOLAS MANNING – (5:281) William Lord, senoir (cuttler) of Salem, with consent of wife, sold to Mr. Nicholas Manning (gunsmith) of Salem for a valuable consideration, a parcel of land both upland & meddow containing ten acres scituate within the township of Salem & comonly knowne by ye name of ye broad field & being bounded as followeth, that is to say, on ye east with ye land of John Pickering, on ye west with ye land belonging to ye Worshipfull Major Hathorne, on ye south side with ye mill river & on the north with ye towne comon. *Signed:* William Lord [mark]; Abigaile Lord [mark]. *Date:* 16 December 1668. *Witnesses:* Benjamin Felton; Edward Norrice. *Acknowledged:* 5:8mo:74 by Abigaile Lord. *Recorded:* 30:11mo:79.

JONATHAN NEALE to BENJAMIN MASTONE – (5:282) Jonathan Neale, (cordwinder) of Salem, sonn of John Neale deceased & heire to the estate of Frances Lawes deceased, for consideration of about 30 pounds in money in hand paid or secured to be paid according to the tenor of a bill given to him by Benjamin Mastone or in his stead by Hilliard Veren Sr. & John Mastone, with free consent of Mary ye now wife of Andrew Mansfield, his honored mother & executrix of ye last will & testament of said Frances Lawes deceased, sold to Benjamin Mastone (merchant) of Salem a certain parcel of land containing about thirty two pole & halfe of ground, being in Salem & pt of that land belonging to ye dwelling house sd Frances Lawes in his life time lived, the dementions of ye said bargained premisses being as followeth. viz: abutting or fronting against ye broad streete that goes from ye meeting house to the town's end westward 4 pole & nine foot in bredth & to run back to the field southward 7 pole or rod of length, same bredth of 4 pole & 9 foot, & it is to be understood ye said nine foot in bredth is by ye Mastone & his successors forever & to be left out towards a highwaye on ye east side, unto which said Jonathan do covenant & promise to and thereto ten foot in bredth more out of own proper interest & propriety & alsoe that there shal be aded & left out nine foot in bredth of ground out of & by any person he shall sell ground to on eastward side of said waye so that there maye be all along the highwaye left through his ground of twenty eight foot wide as he had opportunity to make sale of his said ground which said parcel of land now bargained and sold to ye said Benjamin Mastone lyes bounded easterly by ye said lane or highwaye, soe agreed to be left northerly by the broad streete, westerly & southerly by ye land of said Jonathan Neale & Benjamin Marstone & shall upon his own cost maintaine all the fence that is as partion fences between said Jonathan

& said Benjamin so long as said Jonathan shall keep it in his own hands, the next adjoining land. *Signed:* Jonathan Neale; Mary Neale alias Mansfield [mark]. *Date:* 8 January 1679. Witnesses: Hilliard Veren senior; John Marstone Junior. *Acknowledged:* 13th:11mo:1679 (by Jonathan Neale); 7 June 80 (by Mary Neale alias Mansfield 29 Jul 1680). *Recorded:* 30:11mo:1679.

HENRY BARTHOLMEW to PHILLIP ENGLISH – (5:286) Henry Bartholmew of Salem sold to Phillip English of Salem a parcel of land scituate in the orchard that was sometimes Richard Hollingworth's in Salem & taken & delivered to ye sd Bartholmew by execution, containing in bredth three pole & one quarter at each end & soe runing along by ye side of ye said English his land from end to end through ye said orchard. *Signed:* Henry Bartholmew. *Date:* 17th:8mo:1677. *Witnesses:* Phillip Cromwell; Daniell Weld. *Acknowledged:* 6:12:79. *Recorded:* 9:12:1679. Rec'd £6 in silver upon the account of Mr. Henry Bartholmew of Salem & by his order which is in full sattisfaction of ye land expressed on ye other side by me. *Signed:* Phillip Cormwell. *Date:* 5:Dec:1678. This six pounds abovesd was paid by Phillip English to Phillip Cromwell by my order & is in full payment for the land in ye other side expressed this sixth day of 12mo:1679/80. *Signed:* Henry Bartholmew. *Witness:* Edmond Bridges.

BENJAMIN BROWNE to PHILLIP ENGLISH – (5:288) Benjamin Browne of Salem for diverse good considerations & more especially for a valuable consideratin in hand paid, sold to Phillip English of Salem all his right, title and interest in ye within bargained premisses, according to the tennor of the within deed of sale. *Signed:* Benjamin Browne. *Date:* 9 February 1679/80. *Witnesses:* Hilliard Veren senior; John Moore. *Acknowledged:* 9:12mo:1679. *Recorded:* 9:12:1679. This relates to a deed recorded to ye said Mr. Benj'e Browne in foll. 59 of this booke.

ELEAZER GILES to JOHN KING – (5:289) Eleazer Giles of Salem for consideration of 8 pounds cooper, sold to John King of Salem ten acres of land which his mother gave to him lying in Salem, bounded with lands of Samuell Verrye on west side & the north end & on east side & on south end with his own land & with his brothers. *Signed:* Eleazer Giles. *Date:* 2:day of the 2d month 1663. *Witnesses:* Jokn Deaker; Bethia Perse. *Acknowledged:* 23:4mo:63. *Recorded:* 10:12:1679.

ABRAHAM COLE to WILLIAM BROWNE Jr – (5:289) Abraham Cole (taylor) of Salem owing and being indebted to William Browne Jr. of Salem for sum of 27 pounds to be paid in some good pay, deeded a small dwelling house near to the house he now dwells in which small house he dwelt in

45

before he removed into the house he now dwells in with 9 or 10 pole of land which is fenced in as security for payment. *Signed:* Abraham Cole. *Date:* 3 Mar 1679:80. *Witnesses:* James Powllen; Charles Redford. *Acknowledged:* 4:1mo:79:80. *Recorded:* 4:1mo:1679:80.

ANDREW TARVIS to WILLIAM BRIANT – (5:290) Andrew Tarvis with wife, delivered up all household goods & 2 cows & 2 oxen with all right therein to William Briant. *Signed:* Andrew Tarvis [mark]; Sarah Tarvis [mark]. *Date:* 28, Feb, 1679. *Acknowledged:* 4:1mo:1679:80. *Recorded:* 5:1mo:1679:80.

THOMAS ROOTES Sr & GEORGE HODGES to JOHN LOVETT Jr – (5:291) Thomas Rootes Sr. and George Hodges, both of Salem with consent of wives, Katharen Rootes & Sarah Hodges, for consideration of valuable sum in hand paid, sold to John Lovett Jr of Beverly a small quantity or lot of land about 10 acres in Beverly bounded on northwest with Goodman Hoare's land that now is on the east with Robert Morgaine & on southeast with the sea. *Signed:* Thomas Rootes; George Hodges; Katheren Rootes [mark]; Sarah Hodges [mark]. *Date:* 16 Feb 1679:8[sic]. *Witnesses:* Francis Neale; Josiah Rootes [mark]; John Richards. *Acknowledged:* 17:12mo:79. *Recorded:* 17:12mo:1679.

ROBERT BURNAP Sr to THOMAS CLEARKE – (5:293) Robert Burnap Sr. of Redding for consideration of divers good causes especially 12 pounds, sold to Thomas Clearke 9 acres of meadow in Lynn bounded on north with meadow of Major Holioak, east & west with upland of Maj. Holiock & south with meadow of Robert Burnap Sr. *Signed:* Robert Burnap; Joanah Eaton. *Date:* 24 Aug 1663; *Witness:* William Cowdry. *Acknowledged:* Feb 12:1679 by Robert Burnap; Ann Burnap &Ann gave up dower. *Recorded:* 18:[12mo 1679 crossed out]

JOHN RAMSDELL to AQUILLA RAMSDELL – (5:295) These are to certify this 12 Apr 1675 that it is covenanted between John Ramsdell Sr. of Lynn, husbandman & Aquilla Ramsdell naturall son of John of same town that John, in consideration of his owne, alsoe of his wives inability to carry on & manage their affairs for their comfortable livelihood & that by reason of age hath with consent of wife in surrendering up dower hath made over unto Acquilla to have possession of at death of sd John Ramsdell & his wife they being the natural parents of Aquilla all houselot & housing & orchard, whole being 6 acres abutting easterly on marsh, westerly on land that was Thomas Welman's northerly with country highway & sotherly with land of Richard Haven also 3 acres in same neck of land abutting easterly on marsh of Ensigne Fuller & westerly on land of Mr. Cobbitt northerly on land of

Samuel Hart & southerly on land of Joseph Mansfield also 3 acres of fresh meadow in contrye caled great medow lying betwixt meadow of John Pearson & Joseph Mansfield bounded northerly with marsh of Isaack Hart & southward with upland also 3 acres of fresh meddow lying northwesterly from towne bounded easterly with upland of Richard Haven, westerly with meadow of Joseph Redknap & northerly with upland also 3 acres of salt marsh lying above the bridge bounded easterly with creek or river westerly with upland also 2 acres of salt marsh in 1st division in Rumly marsh being part of 3 acre lot reserving 1 acre; the whole 3 acres being bounded easterly with marsh of Thomas Wheeler westerly with marsh of John Burrill also 1 acre of marsh bounded easterly with mill creek, westerly with upland of Robert Potter, southerly with marsh of Thomas Newhall, northerly marsh of Daniell Gott & his old orchard adjoining land of Richard Hudd & land of or lately of John Gillow bounded southerly with country highway & that Aquila shall manage all business at his own cost & bring in ½ corn & other fruits into barn or dwelling house of John Ramsdell & wife yearly during both their lives...& within 2 years next after both their deaths to pay brother Isaac Ramsdell 2 pounds & within 2 years next after that to pay brother John Ramsdell 5 pounds & so successively to pay each of natural sisters 1 pound a piece, eldest first & so according to age. *Signed:* John Ramsdell Sr [mark]; Aquila Ramsdell [mark]. *Witnesses:* John Fuller; Andrew Mansfield. *Acknowledged:* 21:2mo:77 by both. *Recorded:* 24:12:79.

JOSEPH JENCKES Sr to SAMUELL JENCKES – (5:299) Joseph Jenckes Sr of Lynn for good causes & good afection for his son Samuell Jenckes, 20 acres within the bounds of Lynn bounded northerly by brook & fence next upland which Richard George sometimes held, southwest brook betwixt John Ottaway & it southwesterly lot sometime caled Mr. Rowleses or Mr. Willosses northeasterly a brook & ordain John Floyde of Malden attorney to deliver son possession but reserved use & benefit during life & deed to remain in John Floyd's hands until decease. *Signed:* Joseph Jenckes. *Date:* 24 6mo caled August 1675. *Witnesses:* John Hawkes; Thomas Leonard. *Acknowledged:* by Lt. John Floyd [no date]. *Recorded:* 2:10mo:79.
Richard George & Samuel Apleton saw John Floyd of Malden give Samuell Jenckes quiet possession by turfe & twigg. *Date:* 27:1mo:77. *Signed:* Richard George [mark]; Samuel Apleton; Jon Wilkason [mark]. *Acknowledged:* 27:4mo:79 by John Floyd as aturney to Joseph Jenckes sen'r. *Recorded:* 7:1:1676:77.

HENRY BARTHOLMEW to TIMOTHY LINDALL – (5:302) Henry Bartholmew (merchant) late of Salem, now of Boston, in consideration of 400 pounds sold to Timothy Lindall (merchant) of Salem his dwelling house situate in town of Salem with all ground adjoining thereto containing by estimation one acre of land, of orchard, garden & yards with all outhousing, barns, stables or ware house, fences or appurtenances. Also all that his ware house & wharf by the burying point against the south river, fronting or butting against ye streete northerly & bounded westerly with house & ground of Mr. Nehemiah Willoughby from ye sd streete upon a line directly to ye orchard fence of Nathaniel Pickman & then easterly upon a straite line to ye north east corner of sd Pickman's orchard & thence running upon a straite line on the fence as it stands of ye Pickman's orchard notherly to the common burying place, which bounds that end southerly & bounded easterly with ye land of Mr. John Pilgrim, also sd ware house standing under sd burying point against south river with wharfe. *Signed:* Henry Bartholmew; Elizabeth Bartholmew. Date: 7 February 1679/80. *Witnesses:* Jeremiah Neale; Hilliard Veren, Sr. *Acknowledged:* 26 February 1679 by both & Elizabeth gave consent. *Dower:* Elizabeth freely yielded up her rights. *Recorded:* 4 March 79:80.

WILLIAM BOWDITCH to THOMAS MAULE – (5:306) William Bowditch of Salem acknowledged himself justly indebted unto Thomas Maule of Salem the full & just sum of 51 pounds 11 shillings in current money of New England, for goods bought of him & for sure performance of said debt at or before the first May next, he bound over his ware house and land it stood on with ye wharf that belonged to it which said ware house & land joined to ye south part of ye land of John Pitman & butts upon the south river. *Signed:* William Bowditch. *Date:* 8 March 1679:80. *Witnesses:* William Browne, Jr.; William Murray. *Acknowledged:* 9:first mo. 1679:80. *Recorded:* 9 March 1679:80.

WILLIAM PITT to CHRISTOPHER LATTAMORE & MARY LATTAMORE - (5:307) William Pitt (merchant) of Marblehead for divers good causes and considerations especially a valuable sum sold to Christopher Lattamore (vintner) of Marblehead and his wife Mary, ½ of all that his house & ground lying in Bostone in the county of Suffolke which was the house & ground of Susana his late wife deceased & formerly ye wife of Phillip Eley deceased, bounded with ye land of Gemaliek Waite on ye south east, the land of Amose Richardson to the north west & noreast, common waye or streete on ye south west, the other halfe he having sold to his daughter Grace, ye wife of Thomas Oxford as per deed of sale bearing date with these presents. Christopher Lattamore & Mary engaged to pay father William Pitt for the estate at Bostone when themselves they injoyed it in the behalfe or the whole as above in the 50 shillings the half & 5 pounds the whole. *Signed:* William Pitt; Christopher Lattamore [mark]; Mary

Lattamore. *Date:* 5 Aprill 1679. *Witnesses:* Sam'll Ward; Tho: Parsons; Henry Skerry, senior. *Acknowledged:* 3:5:79. *Recorded:* 10:1mo:1679:80.

HENRY KENEY to THOMAS KENEY – (5:310) Henry Keney (husbandman) of Salem for good causes & considerations, especially fatherly love & affection to Thomas Keney sold him ten acres of land which was adjacent to Thomas' house to begin from Swinertons bounds & soe upon a straite line through the middle of his fower acres of land below his barne & soe to a fallen tree on ye other side of ye sd field & soe from thence to a mark't white oake tree, betwixt sd sonn Thomas & Henry Keney & from that white oake on a straite line to ye above sd Swinertons bounds. Alsoe a piece of swamp in the other side of Nicholses brooke partly cleared. Ye now wife of sd sonn Thomas shall in case son Thomas dy before her injoy ye premises duering ye time of her naturall life & then ye land shall fall to the heires of sd sonn Thomas, in case he hath any heirs then male living, but if not then ye next female heire descending from him, shall injoy the estate during continuance in name Keney but afterwards the sd land & meddow shall fall to next of kin or blood to name Keney & so shall successively descend forever. *Signed:* Henry Keney [mark]. *Date:* 25 September 1679. *Witnesses:* Richard Croade; Frances Croade [mark]. *Acknowledged:* 3:1mo:80. *Recorded:* 11:1mo:1679.

ABRAHAM COLE to SELECTMEN Town of Salem – (5:312) Abraham Cole (taylor) of Salem indebted to the Town of Salem in the sum of 196 pounds 8 shillings 7 pence, upon account of rates as having paid short soe much of severall rates committed to him to gather in year he was constable, deeded his new dwelling house with ye shop & all appurtenances with ye ground yt is there to belonging on ye north side of ye sd house, being parted from ye ground or yard belonging to the old house by a fence, a little distante to ye southward of ye old house: ye sd house & ground bounded with ye broad streete southerly, the lane westerly, his old house & ground northerly & ye land of Edw'd Gaskin easterly. If sd Abraham Cole pay 196 pounds 8 shillings 7 pence at or before 5 Sept next ensuing or provided the Treasurer doe not come upon the Town before for the remainder of the rates for that year, then at or before 25 March 1681 in pay according as the rates for that year was to be pd which payment being well & truly made as aforesaid this sale to be voyde. *Signed:* Abraham Cole. *Date:* 3 March 1679:80. *Witnesses:* Hilliard Veren, senior; Mary Mackmallen [mark]. *Acknowledged:* 4:1mo:1679:80. *Recorded:* 11:1mo:1679.

RICHARD HUCHENSON to SAMUELL LEACH – (5:315) Richard Huchenson of Salem, Administrator to the estate of James Standish deceased, with consent of Sarah his wife, in consideration of 7 pounds, 2 shillings, 6 pence, sold to Samuell Leach (yeoman) of Manchester several parcels of land lying in the bounds of Manchester aforesd formerly the land of James Standish, deceased viz: 1 p'cell of land of seaven acres & a halfe upon ye plaine or elsewhere. Also two acres & a halfe of planting land upon ye neck of land. Alsoe James Standishes share at Skitlen Cove also share in ye fresh meddow. Alsoe one acre & a halfe of swamp or lowlands, lying at the head of ye saw mill cove. Also ye right, title & privilidg of ye sd Standish in or to ye comons or any pt there of alredy devided or shall or may hereafter to be devided of what ye sd Standish formerly bought of Benjamin Parmiter as alsoe all ye aforementioned p'cells or share of land is to be understood of what only the sd Standish formerly bought of ye sd Benjamin Parmiter excepting the acre & halfe of swamp land. *Signed:* Richard Huchenson [mark]; Sarah Huchenson [mark]. *Date:* 25 June 1679. *Witnesses:* Manasses Mastone; Ebenezer Gardner. *Acknowledged:* 16:1mo:79:80 & wife yielded dower. *Recorded:* 16:1mo:1679.

RICHARD HUCHENSON to SAMUELL LEACH & ROBERT LEACH – (5:318) Richard Huchenson of Salem, Administrator of James Standish, deceased, with consent of wife Sarah, in consideration of 40 shillings formerly paid to said James Standish in his life time by Robert Leach of Manchester, deceased, sold to Samuell Leach & Robert Leach, the sons of sd Robert Leach, deceased, one acre of salt marsh lying in bounds of Manchester at Kette cove. *Signed:* Richard Huchenson [mark]; Sarah Huchenson [mark]. *Date:* 15 July 1679. *Witnesses:* Manasseth Mastone; Ebenezer Gardner. *Acknowledged:* 16:1mo:1679:80 Richard Huchenson & Sarah wife owned this...& 2 witnesses sent with wife. *Recorded:* 16:1mo:1679:80.

JOHN MECARTER to HUGH CAMPBELL – (5:319) John Mecarter (dyer) of Salem acknowledged himself to owe & be just indebted unto Hugh Campbell (merchant) of Boston full & just sume of 160 pounds in good currant money & to faithfull payment where of upon demand bound himself, but if the above John Mecarter should pay or cause to be paid the sume of 80 pounds viz: 3 pounds in silver upon 1 Aprill next & to continue quarterly yt is at ye end of every following three months to pay 3 pounds in silver until ye end of three years obligation to be void. *Signed:* John Mecarter [mark]. *Date:* 2 January 1679:80. *Witnesses:* Richard Croad; Frances Croad [mark]. *Acknowledged:* 24:1mo:1679:80. *Recorded:* 24:1mo:79:80. Assignment to George Hacker recorded foll:70 of this book.

JACOB PUDEATER to PEETER CHEEVERS – (5:321) Jacob Pudeater (smith) of Salem with consent of wife, Anne in consideration of a valuable sume of money 9, 14 shillings, 6 pence paid to Mr. Jas. Poland constable of

Salem for his rates, sold to Peeter Cheevers (glover) of Salem smale tract of land & meddow viz: three acres lying together in the northfield Salem & bounded eastward with the land of Mr. Hilliard Veren sen'r & westward with highway, southward with land now in ye possession of Joshua Buffum which was formerly Fermayes & northward with land of Henry Skerry sen'r above mentioned bargained premises was formerly land of Thomas Watson, deceased. *Signed:* Jacob Pudeater [mark]; Ann Pudeater [mark]. *Date:* 20 March 1679/80. *Witnesses:* William Swetland; John Williams. *Acknowledged:* 22:1mo:80 Jacob & Ann his wife, yielded their right in all contained in writing. *Recorded:* 30:March:1680.

ELIZABETH SPOONER to THOMAS FLINT – (5:323) Elizabeth Spooner of Salem administratrix of Thomas Spooner deceased in consideration of 12 pounds sold to Thomas Flint (farmer) of Salem a certain parcel of land containing one halfe acre. Situate and lying in Salem being part of that land or field adjoining to the dwelling house of sd Elizabeth & is bounded on ye north & east with land of sd Elizabeth, with ye streete to south & with a lane that leads to the water side to west & Thomas Flint agreed to set up & maintain partition fence to ye north & east of ye sd premises betweene ye sd halfe acre of land & ye land of ye sd Elizabeth Spooner & that from time to time forever hereafter. *Signed:* Elizabeth Spooner [mark]. *Date:* eleventh day of May 1672. *Witnesses:* Jno Osborne; Daniell Weld. *Acknowledged:* 22:1mo:79:80 by Daniell Weld. *Recorded:* 30 March:1680.

WILLIAM IRELAND Senior to WILLIAM IRELAND – (5:326) William Ireland Senior (yeoman) of Boston for good will and affection he had for son William Ireland deeded all his houses, situate & being att Wills hill, in limits of Salem, being his whole part of the farme formerly Mr. Richard Bellingham's Esq with all the additional land there to by him purchased. Nevertheless, if said sonne William shall at any time during William Senior's naturall life sell sd houses & lands heareby given & granted or any pt there of without his leave or liscence first had & obtained under his hand in writing then this present deed of guift to be of no force. Memorandum before sealing that this instrument is only to ratify & to confirm to sonn William Ireland & daughter upon marriage. *Signed:* William Ireland. *Date:* 4 November 1679. *Witnesses:* Timothy Thorneton; Jeremiah Belcher. *Acknowledged:* March 11:79:80. *Recorded:* 6:April 1680.

MARK HASCALL to JOHN BENETT – (5:329) Mark Hascall (carpenter) of Beverly in consideration of seaventeene shillings sold to John Benett (weaver) of Beverly seaven & twenty pole or thereabouts of upland ground situate in Beverly aforesaid & bounded easterly with land of Richard Haines & with land of same John Benett aforesaid sotherly, with land of Thomas Chubb senior westerly & northerly with the highwaye or common Road. *Signed:* Mark Hascall. *Date:* first day of May 1674. *Witnesses:* Samuell Stackhouse; Richard Woodbury. *Acknowledged:* 10 May 1675. *Recorded:* 10:Aprill:1680.

HUGH CAMPBELL to GEORGE HACKER – (5:330) Hugh Campbell for divers good causes & valuable considerations granted to George Hacker (fisherman) of Salem as well as within written obligation & condition annexed as the sum of 80 pounds also all ye benefit, comodyty penalty & advantage whatsoever which are or hereafter shall grow due unto him from ye within named John Mecarter, his executors, administrators or assigns by virtue or reason of the within written obligation. *Signed:* Hugh Campbell. *Date:* seaventeenth day of Aprill 1680. *Witnesses:* William Paine; Eliezer Woody, serv't; John Hayward, senior. *Acknowledged:* 17th of Aprill. 1680 in Boston. 19:2mo:1680 this assignement refers to the bond recorded in foll:68 in this book and was indorced on ye backside of ye bond.

THOMAS CHUBB to JOHN BENNETT – (5:331) Thomas Chubb (carpenter) of Beverly for consideration of sixteene shillings sold to John Bennett (weaver) of Beverly a small parcel of upland ground containing about sixteene rod or pole situate in Beverly aforesd & bounded northerly & easterly with land of sd John Bennett, sotherly with land of sd Thomas Chubb, westerly with the highwaye or common roade. *Signed:* Thomas Chubb [mark]; Avis Chubb [mark] wife of ye abovesd Thomas Chubb. *Date:* last day of May 1674. *Witnesses:* Samuell Stackhouse; Richard Woodburye. *Acknowledged:* 26 July:78. *Recorded:* 10:Aprill:80.

RICHARD HAYNES to JOHN BENNETT – (5:333) Richard Haynes (husbandman) of Beverly for consideration of 25 pounds sold to John Bennett (weaver) of Beverly five acres of upland ground in Beverly bounded northerly with a piece of land of ye townsmen bought of John Sampson, easterly with ye land of sd Richard Haines, sotherly with ye land of Thomas Chubb senior, westerly with ye land of ye sd John Benett & with ye highwaye or common road. *Signed:* Richard Haines. *Date:* 18 November 1676. *Witnesses:* Richard Poultnoy; Richard Stackhouse. *Acknowledged:* 21:1mo:76:7. *Recorded:* 10:Aprill:80.

JOHN PATCH to JOHN BENNETT – (5:335) John Patch (yeoman) of Beverly for consideration of 20 pounds sold to John Bennett (weaver) of Beverly parcel of upland & swamp ground containing eight acres & three quarters in Beverly bounded easterly with ye land of ye sd John Patch, sotherly with ye land of Richard Patch & westerly with ye land of Samuell Moulton, northerly with ye land of Hugh Woodbery. *Signed:* John Patch [mark]. *Date:* 28th day of December 1677. *Witnesses:* Jonathan Morse; John Richards. *Acknowledged:* 1:11mo:77 & Elizabeth his wife. *Recorded:* 10 Aprill 1680.

ELIZABETH TRASK to JOHN BENNETT – (5:336) Elizabeth Trask (widdow) of Beverly in consideration of a valuable sume sold to John Bennett (weaver) of Beverly one acre & quarter of upland land in Beverly bounded sotherly with ye land of Mark Hascall, westerly and northerly with land of ye sd Elizabeth Trask, easterly with ye highway or common roade. *Signed:* Elizabeth Trask [mark]. *Date:* 26 November 1677. *Witnesses:* Andrew Elliott; Anthony Wood. *Acknowledged:* 1:11mo:77. *Recorded:* 10 Aprill 1680.

WILLIAM HASCALL senior to JOHN BENNETT – (5:338) William Hascall senior (yeoman) of Gloster, chosen by the Court a guardian unto Samuell Hascal, late son of Roger Hascall of Beverly, deceased & also being a feofee in trust for & concerning estate left by ye sd Roger Hascall, deceased unto sd Samuel Hascall in consideration of 14 pounds sterling sold to John Bennett (weaver) of Beverly parcel of upland ground containing two acres in ye towne of Beverly aforesd (and ye sd land formerly pertained of to ye Samuell Hascal's part of his aforesd father Roger's estate per orphanage) & is 5 pole wide, butting upon & bounded by a contry road westward & being in length 60 pole bounded sotherly by a generall field & easterly & northerly bounded by lands pertaining to the orphans of ye sd Roger Hascall, deceased. *Signed:* William Hascall senior [mark]. *Date:* 26 June 1679. *Witnesses:* Samuell Hardie; Samuell West. *Acknowledged:* 26:4mo:79. *Recorded:* 10 Aprill 1680.

THOMAS COOPER to SAMUEL SOTHWICK – (5:340) Thomas Cooper (husband.) of Salem in consideration of 45 pounds silver sold to son in law Samuel Sothwick the whole and every part of the dwelling house in Salem & which heretofore was the house, he said the dwelling house of his predecessor John Sothwick, now by him dwelt in & his rightful estate by virtue of his marrying with Sarah, the relict of ye sd John Southwick together with his right title & estate property & interest in & unto ye lands of the said John Sothwick. That is to say the right of widdowes thirds by law due unto his pre'sent sd wife & as executrix in & unto ye this sd estate in lands, meaning yt he does by these pr'sents freely & absolutely sell & confirme unto ye aforesd Samuell Sothwick the sd dwelling house as also the thirds in ye sd land due Samuel as an heire to his aforesd father John Sothwick's estate together with the right of thirds which will be do unto the brothers of ye sd Samuell viz: John & Isaac Sothwick when they come to age, in the mean time & ever after during ye time of ye naturall life of aforesd wife alsoe title, priviledge & interest in & unto ye halfe of the estate in lands, the halfe barne which will be due unto John Sothwick & Isaac Sothwick his brother when they come of age at present in Thomas' possession provided & agreed upon that Thomas Cooper aforesd shall have to his owne use the estward end of ye dwelling house aforesd & also shal have liberty to take of from the land aforesd firewood necessary & convenient for his own particular use & likewise aforesd Samuell Sothwick nor any one else by his order or allowance shall not make stay or wast of any of the wood or timber on yt pt of ye land which belongs to sd brother John & Isaac Sothwick, the firewood aforesd ye sd Thomas Cooper is to have only during ye space of two years from the date heareof & like wise ye eastward end of ye sd house for the same time beginning from ye date hearof but in case Thomas Cooper did not live in ye sd house himselfe nor his wife, if in case he should remove to any other place or dy before, Thomas Cooper shall not let out sd house to rent to any one elce but Samuel Sothwick shall have it. *Signed:* Thomas Cooper; Sarah Cooper [mark]. *Date:* 15 March 1679:80. *Witnesses:* Thomas Preston; Richard Croad; Thomas Fuller, guardian of John Sothwick. *Acknowledged:* 25:1:80 by Tho. Cooper & Sarah wife. *Recorded:* 12 April 1679.

JEREMIAH MEACHUM senior to GEORGE HACKER & BETHIAH HACKER – (5:344) Jeremiah Meachum senior (fuller) of Salem for good will & natural affection he bore unto him gave to his son in law George Hacker and wife Bethiah his daughter of Salem a certain parcel of land containing fouerteene pole or rod of ground lying at the townes end, neere the bridg or casewaye without the fortification upon which sd land ye said George Hacker have late built a smale dwelling house bounded on the north river with a highwaye northwesterly, by ye land of his northeast & alsoe southeast & highwaye or street southwest. *Signed:* Jeremiah Meachum [mark]; Margarett Meachum [mark]. *Date:* 4 March 1679:80. *Witnesses:* William Gill; William Pensent. *Acknowledged:* 16:2mo:1680. *Recorded:* 16 April:79.

ROBERT BRETT to HENRY BARTHOLMEW – (5:346) Robert Brett (planter) of Salem in consideration of 7 pounds 10 shillings sold to Henry Bartholmew of Salem the one halfe of ye two acres of land that ye sd Robert Brett bought of William Lord of Salem being sometime ye land of Mr. Webb of Linden, scituate between ye land of Nathanyel Pitnam on ye west & of William Golt & John Miller on ye east, butting upon ye burying place & thence up to the streete, the said halfe part being that halfe part on ye westerly side running from ye streete down to ye burying place, next unto ye land of ye sd Henry Bartholmew & Nathanyell Pitnam. *Signed:* Robert Brett. *Date:* 9th day of ye sixth month 1655. *Witnesses:* John Browne; John Fiske. *Acknowledged:* 22 July 1680. *Recorded:* 22 July 1680.

Nathanell Putnam senior made oathe yt neere about ye time of ye date of the above written yt he did by order of Mr. Robert Britt measured out & delivered unto Mr. Henry Bartholmew the land above exsprest in the deed 21:July.

John Browne & John Fisk made oath as witnesses 22 Jul 1680 entered as a caution.

HENRY WEST to JOHN MARSTON Junior – (5:347) Henry West (sadler) of Salem for a valuable consideration paid in hand sold to John Marston, Junior (carpenter) of Salem a certain parcel of ground lately given him by ye towne of Salem with a dwelling house standing upon it, ground containing two or three pole as it was bounded out by the towne & scittuate in Salem neere the meeting house & bounded on ye west with ye land of Ralph Fogg, on ye north & east with ye common land or streete, on ye south with some land either common land or appertaining to Thomas Tuck lately. *Signed:* Henry West; Elizabeth West [mark]. *Date:* 16 August 1671. *Witnesses:* Hilliard Veren, senior; William Dounton; Hilliard Veren junior; John Price. *Acknowledged:* 20 Aprill:1680 by Henry West & his wife Elizabeth. *Recorded:* 20 Aprill 1680.

JOHN RUCK senior to JOHN MARSTON Junior – (5:349) John Ruck senior (merchant) of Salem in consideration of 10 pounds sold to John Marston Junior (carpenter) of Salem one half acre of land scituat in ye towne of Salem & is part of that field yt did belong to sd John Ruck & adjoining to his dwelling house bounded with a lane or highwaye that runs from a cove yt comes out of ye south river to the common, commonly called Lawes hill on ye north & also with a little cove coming out of another place of ye south river south & some land of Mathew Woodwell to ye east and some land of Eleazer Gedney to the west. *Signed:* John Ruck; Elizabeth Ruck. *Date:* 19 Aprill 1680. *Witnesses:* Hilliard Veren senior; Thomas Andrew; Benjamin Marston with seizin & possession given. *Acknowledged:* 20th of Aprill:1680. *Recorded:* 20:Aprill:1680.

THOMAS ROOTES senior & CATHERINE ROOTE with GEORGE HODGES – (5:351) Thomas Rootes senior & wife made agreement with George Hodges that whereas Thomas Rootes & wife by reason of age & weakness of body are not able by their labour to provide for theire comfortable livelihood as formerly do therefore covenant & agree with George Hodges to keep & maintain them ye sd Thomas Rootes & his wife the whole time of their naturall lives with victuals, cloathes, firing, phissick & tendance as theire conditions shall require in consideration of which ye sd George Hodges is to have the use & improvement of ye whole estate of ye said Thomas Rootes during the whole time of the naturall lives of ye sd Thomas Rootes & his wife excepting thirty pole of land on the southwest corner of his homelott that is to say five pole broad next by ye towne comon & six pole long next Mr. Bartholmew's pasture which ye sd Thomas Rootes reserves for a house lott for Catherine Hodges if she shall have occasion of it. & if not then George Hodges is to have ye thirty pole of land & pay unto his daughter Catherine the full value of it: alsoe ye sd Thomas Rootes reserves unto his own proper use & for the use of his wife theire best lower roome together with theire beding, chests & cloathing & household stuff which is theirin at the sealing of this agreement to be at theire own dispose during the time of theire naturall lives & att their decease then what shall be left of the moveables shall fall to Catherine Hodges as a particular portion for hers & also at decease of Thomas Rootes & his wife then there whol estate which now George Hodges is possest of together with their best lower room shall then fall to George Hodges to be his own proper right but in case it shall please God to take away George Hodges before Thomas Rootes & his wife then this agreement is to stand voyde & successors of George Hodges shall have full satisfaction made them for what charge George Hodges have been out about ye sd Rootes & his wife which shal be judged by Mr. Hen: Bartholmew senior, Samuell Gardner senior, Samuell Gardner Junior or any two of them unto whose judgment they do ingage to abide, also if at any time there shall difference arise between them which they canot end amongst themselves, then it is by these presents declared by joynt consent of both parties that the three men before mentioned or any two of them shall heare & determine all such difference & if any one of ye three men before named be removed by death or any other means whereby he canot act in the pr'misses either in awarding what satisfaction the heirs & secessors of George Hodges shall have then it shal be in ye liberty of the other two to make choice of one they shall judg meete to joyn with them. *Signed:* Thomas Rootes; George Hodges; Catherine Roote [mark]. *Date:* 12th day of Aprill 1680. *Witnesses:* Sam'll Gardner senior; Sam'll Gardner Junior. *Recorded:* 12:3mo:1680.

SAMUELL GARDNER & EBENEZER GARDNER – (5:354) Samuell Gardner & Ebenezer Gardner, executors of the last will & testament of honored father George Gardner, late deceased, assigned, ordained & made & in their steed & place trusted & wel beloved friend Caleb Stanly of Hartford Ct & in their names as executors to be their true & lawfull attorney & to ask, sue fore, levy, require, recover & receive of all & every p'son or p'sons in their name in or neere sd colony all & every such debts, rents &

sumes of money, marchandise & other goods, as are now due unto us or shall be due. *Signed:* Samuell Gardner; Ebenezer Gardner. *Date:* 24th day of May 1680. *Witnesses:* John Price; John Hathorne. *Acknowledged:* 24:May 1680. *Recorded:* 24:May:1680.

RICH'D WALKER to JOHN LEGG – (5:355) Mr. Rich'd Walker (yeoman) of Linn for divers good & valuable causes sold to Mr. John Legg (shoemaker) of Marblehead one hundred areas of upland & seaven acres of fresh meddow within ye bounds of Redding bounded as followeth: ye south side by a river called Bare meddow & by ye east side by Capt George Cornell's farme & by ye north side by ye river & by the west side bounded by Redding commons, & ye seaven acres of meddow lying right opposite against ye sd hundred of upland over a river known & called by ye name of Bare river with all woods, underwoods, trees, timber, pasture, meddows, marshes, feedings ponds, waters, swamps, mines... *Signed:* Richard Walker. *Date:* 6th day of May 1680. *Witnesses:* Walter Phillips; Daniell King. *Acknowledged:* 8:June:1680 by Capt. Richard Walker. *Recorded:* 8:June:80.

PEETER BRACKETT – (5:357) Whereas there was a house & land which he bought of Samuell Belknap which lay in his hands for the payment of 47 pounds to be pd unto Peeter Brackett of Boston that the sd money was paid & satisfied unto Mr. Peeter Brackett by Thomas Maule of Salem. *Signed:* Peeter Brackett. *Acknowledged:* June 18:1680.
This relates to deed entered in foll 66.

HENRY TREVETT, senior to RICHARD KNOTT – (5:358) Henry Trevett (fisherman) of Marblehead in consideration of a certaine sum of money sold to Richard Knott (cherurgeon) of Marblehead a certain parcel of land in Marblehead incloased in a stone wale fence containing about halfe an acre bounded by ye highwaye on ye south side & on ye north bounded on ye land of ye sd Knott & ye easter side of ye sd land joyneth on ye land yt was Walter Beastons also on which land standeth the house which Elias White had leave to sett up & now in ye possession of ye abovesd Richard Knott. *Signed:* Henry Trevett. *Date:* 7 April 1680. *Witnesses:* John Leach; Robert Nicholson; Nicholas Pickett [mark]. *Acknowledged:* 15 June 1680. *Recorded:* 15 June 1680.

NICHOLAS MANNING to JEREMIAH NEALE – (5:360) Nicholas Manning (gunsmith) of Salem for consideration of 200 pounds & silver & other pay, sold to Jeremiah Neale (carpenter) of Salem his dwelling house, messuage, shopps & housing to sd messuage & dwelling house appertaining upon which ye sd house & housing stands containing in ye whole about an acre of ground scittuate in Salem aforesd bounded easterly upon ye streete & highwaye, westerly upon ye land of John Gedney, northerly upon the land of John Preist & Samuell Beadle & sotherly upon the land of Mr. Wm Browne senior & John Gedney. *Signed:* Nicholas Manning. *Date:* 1 September 1675. *Witnesses:* Nathaniel Beadle; Samuell Beadle. *Acknowledged:* 17 June 1680. *Recorded:* 18 June 1680. There is an instrument recorded in the 6th book page ye 25th whereby this above pr'tended conveyance is declared & made null by ye sd Jeremiah Neale.

MARY PORTER to THO. GARDNER Junior – (5:362) Mary Porter, relict & executrix of John Porter of Salem (yeoman) deceased, in consideration of a valuable sum, sold to son-in-law Tho. Gardner junior (marchant) of Salem a certain parcell of ground in Salem by ye south river at the burying point, it being a parcel of land formerly granted by the towne of Salem to ye John Porter when they granted severall other parcells to severell other men for wharfing & building warehouses & ye sd parcell contained 35 foot in front or bredth against the water bounding easterly upon Major Wm. Hathornes grant east & bounded by ye grant of Samuell Gardner & Capt Joseph Gardner west. *Signed:* Mary Porter [mark]. *Date:* 15 June 1680. *Witnesses:* John Porter; Abraham Browne. *Acknowledged:* 16 June 1680. *Recorded:* 18 June 1680.

ROBERT BRIDGES to ISAACK HART – (5:364) Robert Bridges (gentleman as aturney to Capt Edward Tomlins gentleman of London, late of Linn) of Lynn, county of Midlesex in consideration of 13 pounds, sold to Isaack Hart (husbandman) of Redding all that farme of two hundred acres of land, together with the premisses & every of the appurtenances thereunto belonging, scituate in ye bounds of ye towne of Linn the which sd farme was given to ye sd Edward Tomlins & laid out by ye sd towne: as also ye sd Robert Bridges as aturney aforesd doth hearby make over unto ye sd Isaack Hart, all the right said Edward Tomlins hath in any meddow ground (over & besides the said two hundred acres) of any such meddow of ye sd Edward Tomlins has within two miles of ye sd farms. *Signed:* Robert Bridges. *Date:* 28:5mo:1649. *Witnesses:* Mary Bridges; [Toll/Tolt?] *Acknowledged:* 21:6:1656 by Capt. Robert Bridges. *Recorded:* 21 June 1680. Robert Bridges acknowledged that about last day of November 1649 there was received in wheate 13 pounds. *Signed:* Robert Bridges.

JOHN RUCK Senior to JOSEPH MANSFEILD Sr. – (5:366) John Ruck Senior (marchant) of Salem in consideration of sume of 30 pounds sterling sold to Joseph Mansfeild, Sr. (yeoman) of Linn all that messuage or tenement of his situate in ye town of Linn aforesd containing two acres of land with a dwelling house standing thereupon which was the house &

ground formerly sold by Nathaniell Kirtland to Joseph Armitage & since recovered by ye said John Ruck by cource of law & virtue of an execution, levied thereupon, apprised delivered unto him for his uses benefitts & behoofe forever as may appear by Salem Court records & is or late was in ye tenure & occupation of John Longly as his tenent of sd house & land, being bounded easterly with ye house lott of Thomas Townsend, westerly with ye land of ye sd Nathaniell Kirtland, northerly with ye mill streete & sotherly with ye land of Thomas Townsend & Nathaniell Kirtland. *Signed:* John Ruck; Eliza: Ruck. Wife Elizabeth consented & yielded dower. *Date:* 17 June 1678. *Witnesses:* John Ruck Junior; Tho. Ruck; Andrew Mansfeild; Mary Mansfeild [mark]. *Acknowledged:* 17:4mo:78. *Recorded:* 16:5mo:1680.

JOHN GROVER to ANTHONY WOOD – (5:369) John Grover (husbandman) of Beverly in consideration of 5 pounds and 10 shillings sold to Anthony Wood (weaver) of Beverly one acre of upland ground scituate in Beverly bounded easterly & sotherly with ye land of Edmond Grover, northerly with ye land of Roger Hascall senior, westerly with ye land of John Conant senior & with ye land of ye sd Anthony Wood. *Signed:* John Grover; Edmund Grover [mark]. *Date:* 29 June 1678. *Witnesses:* John Benet; John Davis [mark]. *Acknowledged:* 29:day of June:1678. *Recorded:* 16:5:80.

JEREMIAH BELCHER senior & MARY BELCHER to JOSEPH HARDY Jr. – (5:370) Jeremiah Belcher senior of Ipswich and wife, Mary in consideration of 12 pounds sold to Joseph Hardy Jr. (marrenor) of Salem a parcel of upland to the continent of about two hundred & twenty acres scituate neare to Merremack river on the northerne side in county of Essex, alsoe 20 acres of meddow lying about a mile distant from ye sd land on the side ye sd land being bounded as followeth viz: one hundred & twenty poles bredth in ye front upon ye river ranging sotherly upon ye westerne side of the land which I have sold to James Polen three hundred & twenty pole in length butts on ye common northerly & on ye other side ye same length of three hundred & twenty poles ranging upon ye comon. *Signed:* Jeremiah Belcher; Mary Belcher [mark]. *Date:* 13 July 1680. *Witnesses:* James Powllen; Richard Croades. *Acknowledged:* 13:of July:1680 by both. *Recorded:* 15:July:1680.

DAVID PERKINS to ROBERT ROUNDY – (5:373) David Perkins (smith) of Beverly for consideration of 85 pounds sold to Robert Roundy (husbandman) of Beverly one acre of land scituate in ye towne of Beverly bounded sotherly with ye land of John Stone, northerly by ye land of John Trask, westerly by ye land of Mark Hascal & easterly by ye highwaye, with a dwelling house standing upon ye sd land. *Signed:* David Perkins. *Date:* fifth of May 1680. *Witnesses:* Samuell Hardy; John Band. *Acknowledged:* 25 June:1680. Elizabeth ye wife of David Perkins acknowledged & consented & surrendered thirds 25 June 1680. *Recorded:* 22:July:1680.

THOMAS HAINES to DAVID PERKINS – (5:375) Thomas Haines (malster) of Salem village for consideration of 70 pounds stirling sold to David Perkins (blacksmith) of Beverly a certain parcel of land containing seaven acres scituate within ye town of Beverly bounded westerly by ye land of John Benett, northerly by ye land of Mr John Hale & ye land of John Sampson, easterly by ye highwaye & ye land of the said Sampson, sotherly by ye land of Thomas Chub senior & eight acres more of ground in ye towne of Beverly aforesd bounded westerly by ye land of John Lambert, northerly by ye land of Josiah Rootes, easterly by ye lands of William Dixy and William Stackhouse & sotherly by ye river & ye land of William Bath which sd parcels of land did formerly with ye comonige thereto p'taine unto Richard Haines late of Beverly & was by him given & sett over unto Thomas Haines. Also Richard Haines above mentioned as former owner of ye bargained premises, before his alienation there of aforesd, approved of, confirmed unto ye said David Perkins all the right & interest which he had or heare after might or should have in ye sd lands & comonage. *Signed:* Thomas Haines; Raynes Haynes. *Date:* tenth day of Aprill 1680. *Witnesses:* Joshua Rea; Samuell Hardie. *Acknowledged:* 5:3mo:1680 & wife Sara yielded right. *Recorded:* 22:July:1680.

THOMAS WHEELER to WILLIAM BASSETT Senior – (5:378) Thomas Wheeler (yeoman) of Stonington in New England in consideration of a full & valuable sume of money sold to William Bassett senior (yeoman) of Linn nine acres of fresh meddow in that meddow usually called Reedy meddow being within the bounds of Linn lying northerly upon Rob't Bales his upland, easterly upon Richard Haven senior his meddow, sotherly with great brooke, westerly with ye land of Daniell Eatten. *Signed:* Thomas Wheeler. *Date:* 28 June 1680. *Witnesses:* John Fuller; John Newhall. *Acknowledged:* June ye 30:1680. *Recorded:* 22 July 1680.

BRIAN PENNELTON to WILLIAM DODGE Senior, JOHN RAYMENT Sen'r, WILLIAM RAYMENT – (5:381) Brian Pennelton of Sacoe In province of Maine at the request of William Dodg senior, John Rayment Sen'r and William Rayment of Beverly acknowledged that about the yeare of one thousand six hundred & fifty three or fifty four did make sale of certaine farme at Topsfield containing about six hundred acres of land upland & meddow with ye housing upon it, which farme had formerly belonged unto Old Mr. Thomas Dudley & after that belonged to Mr.

Whittingham of Ipswich of whom sd Brian Pennelton bought it & afterwards sold it as above said to sd William Dodg Sen'r, John Rayment sen'r & William Rayment & company & gave a deed of sale. *Signed:* Brian Pennelton. *Date:* 30:day of July:1680. *Acknowledged:* 30:4mo:1680 Major Brian Pennelton owned before the Justices at theire Sessions & at Court of Pleas declared this his act & deed. *Signed:* John Scottom Justice in behalfe & per order of rest of Justices for province of Maine. Entered into records of Province of Maine 1st day of July 1680. *Recorded:* 28:July:1680.

NICHOLAS MANING to JOHN BROWNE Senior; HENRY BARTHOLMEW – (5:382) Nicholas Maning (gunsmith) of Salem in consideration of 52 pounds sold to John Browne senior (ruling elder of the Church of Salem) & Mr. Henry Bartholmew (merchant) of Salem – overseers & feofees in trust for the children of Mr. Robert Graye of Salem lately deceased, one dwelling scituate in Salem late in tenure of sd Robert Graye together with an acre of ground thereunto belonging & adjoining bounded on ye south with ye land of Mr. William Browne senior, merchant, on the north with ye land of ye R. Worshipfull John Endicot Esq the Honored Govenor, on ye west with ye land of Mr. Gedney senior & on ye east with ye lane or highwaye, provided if sd Nicholas Manning repay sd Mr. John Browne & Mr. Henry Bartholmew ovseers & feofees in trust as aforesd sd 52 pounds for the use & benefit of ye children of Mr. Robert Grey, lately deceased as by his last will & testament hath beene and is ordered & appointed upon any demands or within six months after it shal be lawfully demanded, in good merchantable or refuse fish or in sugar at price current that then this sale to be voyd. *Signed:* Nicholas Maning. *Date:* 14 March 1663/4. *Witnesses:* Joseph Grafton; Edward Norrice. *Acknowledged:* 29:4mo:1680 Nicholas Manning owned above & sd he thought this to be his hand. The Court allowed above written to be a legall acknowledgement. *Recorded:* 30:4mo:1680.

JEREMIAH NEALE to FRANCIS NICHOLLS – (5:384) Jeremiah Neale (carpenter) of Salem for valuable consideration sold to Francis Nicholls (joyner) of Salem a parcel of upland containing by estimate two acres scituate in ye sd towne of Salem by ye north river side bounded on ye north & west sides thereof by ye sd river it being a point of land shooting out ye waye on ye west with ye lane or waye highwaye which lyeth between ye sd ground & ye land of Marshall Henry Skerry & on ye south with some land of his own & p'tly with ye land of Mr. John Smith, maulster, provided & it is agreed between ye parties that ye sd Jeremiah Neale shall & may at all times have free liberty without interruption or any molestation from ye sd Francis Nicholls or any other p'son or p'sons by their means consent or procurement to land or cause to be landed any timber or other wood upon the banke between ye sd lane & ye nearest point of sd land or to build any smale vessel or cause it to be built upon ye sd bankes side. *Signed:* Jeremiah Neale. *Date:* 10 June 1673. *Witnesses:* Thomas Whitned; Edward Norrice senior. *Acknowledged:* 6:6mo:1677. *Recorded:* 29 July 1680.

JOHN WILKINSON & JOHN PROVENDER to HENRY ROADES –

(5:386) John Wilkinson of Maulden & John Provender of Maulden acknowledged themselves to be indebted unto Mr. Henry Roades of Lynn of ye full & just sume of nine pounds, seaven shillings & 6 pence as soe much being lent to them in current lawfull money due to be paid to him in current lawfull money or to his order or assignes the ninth day of March next ensueing ye date heare of at ye dwelling house of ye said Henry Roades in Linn & for the due & true payment of ye sd moneyes, both for quantity, time & place of payment as abovesd ye aforesd John Wilkenson & John Provender made over unto ye aforesd Henry Roades two acres of salt marsh ground abating twenty pole, which marsh in ye first division of Rumney marsh which was lately in the possession of John Wilkenson senior father unto ye abovesd John Wilkenson and in ye township of Linn for him to have the produce of for pr'sent yeare viz: one acre & a quarter bounded easterly with ye marsh of Mr. Samuell Whiting, westerly with ye marsh of Nathaniell Kirtland southwardly with ye lower division of lotts & northwardly with ye marsh of Abraham Wilkenson & half an acre of it & twenty rod bounded easterly with the marsh of Mr. Samuell Whiting & westerly of Nathanniell Kirtland, sothwardly with ye marsh of Isaac Wilkenson & northwardly with ye marsh of Samuell Howard being understood that in case ye aforesd sume of money be not pd as before at or before ye ninth day of March next ensuing ye date heare of then ye aforesaid two acres, bate twenty poles they for ye sd sume of money sell & convey unto sd Henry. *Signed:* John Wilkenson [mark]; John Provender [mark]. *Date:* 9 March 1676:77. *Witnesses:* Andrew Mansfield; Samuell Roades. *Acknowledged:* 14:2mo:16:77. *Recorded:* 29:July:80.

THOMAS GREENE to REMEMBER SAMONS - (5:388) Thomas

Greene (husbandman) of Salem in consideration of 12 pounds due unto Remember Samons as per Court order doe & may appeere sold to Remember Samons (widdow) of Salem a p'cell of land containing ten acres as it was laid out & granted to him by ye towne of Salem within ye bounds of sd towne neere unto a farm called Mr. Humphries farme & bounded northward with ye land John Pudney beginning at walnut tree being corner bounds at ye northwest from thence to an oake at ye northeast corner standing by a great rock, from thence to a black oake marked on ye foure sides at ye southeast corner joining to the common from thence bounded to ye common on ye southwest side to a walnut tree that is marked with fourer markes & from thence to ye first bounds. *Signed:* Thomas Greene [mark]. Wife does yield all her right title dower or interest {text indicated that wife was to sign but no signature for her.} *Date:* first day of October 1678. *Witnesses:* John Endicot; Steven Sewall; William Dounton. *Acknowledged:* 24:of November. 1679. *Recorded:* 29:July:1680.

REMEMBER SAMONS to JOHN CROMWELL – (5:391) Remember Samons (widdow) of Salem in consideration of 10 pounds sold to John Cromwell (slaughterer) of Salem a p'cell of land containing ten acres as was laid out & granted to Mr. Thomas Greene by ye towne of Salem within the bounds of ye sd towne, neere unto a farme called Mr. Humfrys farme & bounded northward with ye land of John Pudney being at a walnut tree, being John Pudney's corner bounds at ye northwest from thence to an oake at ye northeast corner standing by a great rock from thence to a black oake marked on the four sides at ye southeast corner joining to the comon, from thence bounded to ye comon on ye southwest side to a walnut tree that is marked with four markes & from thence to ye first bound. *Signed:* [no signature]. *Date:* 29 Aprill 1680. *Witnesses:* Michaell Darich [mark]; Elizabeth Stacye [mark]. *Acknowledged:* 30:2mo:1680. *Recorded:* 29: July:1680.

JEREMIAH BELCHER to PHILLIP CROMWELL – (5:393) Jeremiah Belcher (yeoman) of Ipswich in consideration of a valuable sume sold to Phillip Cromwell (slautherer) of Salem a p'cell of upland & meddow containing by measure & judgment four hundred & fifty acres scittuate neere to ye bounds of Haverill line in New England bounded by a pond formerly his, given to John Cromwell & soe is now commonly called by the name of Cromwell's pond, on ye sotherne side of ye farme of the Reverend Mr Thomas Cobbett on ye western side upon Haverill line on ye eastern side & on ye land which sometimes was William Reeves now John Cromwell's land on the northerne side. *Signed:* Jeremiah Belcher; Mary Belcher [mark]. *Date:* 3 May 1680. *Witnesses:* James Powllen; Hugh Gallowaye [mark]. *Acknowledged:* June:21:1680 by Sargt Jeremiah Belcher. Mary, his wife did freely surrender her thirds. *Recorded:* 29:July:1680.

JEREMIAH BELCHER to JOHN CROMWELL – (5:396) Sargt Jeremiah Belcher of Ipswich for valuable consideration sold to John Cromwell (slatherer) of Salem a p'cell of upland & meddow containing by estimate two hundred fifty acres scituat neere to ye bounds of Haverill in New England & about eight miles from the meeting house of ye sd Haverill

& is ye same p'cell of land which he formerly engaged & sett unto William Reeves for a debt due by him to ye sd Reeves but the sd debt being discharged ye afore sd land was again in his possession & bounded both for ye land & meddow by the west on Mr. Cobbitt's farme, on ye east by Haverill line, on ye south by Mr. Phillip Cromwell's land which was also formerly his & sold unto the sd Mr. Phillip Cromwell & soe goes northerly so fare until the compliment of two hundred & fifty acres of upland & meddow according, to the true & faithfull intent heare of be made up & acknowledged to have sold unto ye sd John Cromwell all his land & meddow in ye place afore sd & received full satisfaction for it, all his land theire lying to the northward of ye land which was William Reeve from ye sd Cromwell's pond to Mr. Thomas Cobbitts line & soe to ye west as farr as his land went with all his whole right. *Signed:* Jeremiah Belcher; Mary Belcher [mark]. *Date:* 3 May 1680. *Witnesses:* James Powllen; Hugh Gallowaye [mark]. *Acknowledged:* June:21:1680 by Sargt Jeremy Belcher & Mary his wife did freely surrender her thirds. *Recorded:* 29:July:1680.

JOHN BROWNE Sen'r to HANA/HANNA/HANNAH BROWNE – (5:399) John Browne Sen'r (marriner) of Salem for divers good causes & considerations especially for that love & good will which he had & bore unto Hana Browne, widow, his daughter in law late wife of his sonn James Browne deceased, gave granted & confirmed unto ye sd Hanna Browne all that his part of ye dwelling house where ye said Hannah Browne lived in & had beene & was possessed of which was all ye eastward part of ye sd house together with a yard belonging there as it was fenced in & alsoe in her possession. Alsoe a little garden in her possession which sd garden contained four pole of ground as fenced in & bounded with a lane that ran between John Archard & ye sd Browne's house in ye tenure of Robert Hodge westerly, & the garden of ye sd Browne on ye north & his orchard on ye east & his land belonging to ye house aforesaid ye sd Hodge lived in to the south all ye sd housing & premises being in Salem. *Signed:* John Browne Sen'r. *Date:* third March 1679/80. *Witnesses:* Richard Taley; Elizabeth Gardner. *Acknowledged:* 27 July:1680. *Recorded:* 29 July 1680.

JOSEPH BOYCE Sr to THOMAS MAULE, JOSIAH SOTHWICK Sr, JOHN SMALL, JOHN BURTON Sr, & DANIELL SOTHWICK – (5:402) Joseph Boyce Sr, (tanner) of Salem, for consideration of 5 pounds, sold to Thomas Maule, Josiah Sothwick Sr, John Small, John Burton Sr & Daniell Sothwick, all of Salem, a parcel of land in Salem, 16 poles more or less bounded & fenced, part of land now adjoining his dwelling house, bounded easterly, westerly & southerly by land of John Boyce & northerly by highway, so called or common land, for the proper use of a burying place. *Signed:* Joseph Boyce [mark]. *Date:* 10 June 1680. *Witnesses:* Ann

Nedom; Provided Gaskill. Possession given by turf & twig 3rd day of 6th mo 1680. **Recorded:** 14:6:1680.

EDWARD TOMLINS to JONATHAN PALMES – (5:405) Edward Tomlins (gentleman) of Dublin ordained his well beloved friend Jonathan Palmes (gentleman) of Clearwell, Ireland to be true and lawful attorney in his name and to his use to ask, sue for, levy & to recover & receive of every person whatsoever in New England for all & every such debts, sums or land or money as are now due unto him either by bond, bill or otherwise or which shall be due by any manner of meanes whatsoever giving said attorney full power & authority in & about premises & upon receipt of any such debt or sum of money discharges in his name & to make & deliver all & every act in the law necessary to be done in or about premises for recovery of any such sums of money & in his name to do execute & perform in every respect as he could do if personally present. *Signed:* Edw Tomlins. *Date:* 20 August 1679. *Witnesses:* John Palmer; John Ogden; Amos Ogden; Nathaniell Mather. *Acknowledged:* Lord Mayor of City of Dublin Peter Ward certified that day within named Edward Tomlin signed within letter of aturney & he certified & caused seal of office of mayoralty of city to be affixed 22 August 1670 Signed Peeter Ward. *Recorded:* 14:6:1680.

JONATHAN PALMER to Capt. THOMAS MARSHALL – (5:407) Jonathan Palmer (merchant) of Boston & attorney of Edward Tomlins (gentleman) of Dublin Ireland for consideration of 40 pounds, sold to Capt. Thomas Marshall of Linn all several parcels of land granted to Edward Tomlins by the town of Linn in 1638 & 1651 lying within bounds of Linn both upland & meadow according to records of said town grants. To have all above parcels & all other lands belonging to Edward Tomlins within the bounds of Linn. *Signed:* Jonathan Palmer. *Date:* 15 June 1680. *Witnesses:* Ralph King; Is^a Addington. *Acknowledged:* 16 June 1680. *Recorded:* 14:6:1680.

FRANCES JOHNSON to THOMAS HAWKINS – (5:409) Frances Johnson of Boston, with consent of wife, Hanna, for consideration of a certain sum of money, sold to Thomas Hawkins (tailor) of Marblehead one messuage, tenement or dwelling house with land enclosed with a stone wale upon which house stands with two cowes leases on comons which house, land, & comons are situate & being in Marblehead. *Signed:* Francis Johnson; Hannah Johnson. Wife Hanah yielded dower. *Date:* 31 May 1679. *Witnesses:* John Turner; Samuell Morgaine. *Acknowledged:* 31 3 1679 by both. *Recorded:* 18:6:1680.

Captain JAMES OLIVER to NATHANIEL BARNES – (5:411) Captain James Oliver of Boston, for consideration of several sums of money at sundry times paid & 10 pounds, sold to Nathaniel Barnes of Boston moiety or half part of a tract or piece of land lying with the bounds of Linn containing 350 acres granted by town unto father in law Thomas Dexter in 1638 & by him conveyed by deed dated 11 May 1675 unto him & his brother Richard, wood which remains still undivided with all his estate rights to a parcel of land at a place called Nahant neere Linn. *Signed:* James Oliver. *Date:* 14 June 1680. *Witnesses:* Joseph Bridgham; Wm Hoare. *Acknowledged:* August 23, xxiii. *Recorded:* 31 August 1680.

STEPHEN HASKETT to EDMUND WHARTON – (5:414) Stephen Haskett (merchant) of Salem for consideration of 10 pounds sterling sold to Edmund Wharton (glasier) of Salem a certain piece of ground lately bought from William Lord Sr. by deed dated 6 April 1664 lying in Salem adjoining to & being part of ground on which house of William Lord stands bounded with the south river to the south & land of William Lord to the north, on east bounded with a stake driven down close to the railes of Mr. Elias Stileman adjoining to his ground being four in foot & two or three inches wide between the stake & John Coles len too stone wale & from that stake it runs next adjoining land of William Lord westerly to a stake drove down against a post westward which is fifty foot & a half or there about between the two stakes, & from east it carries breadth of four foot & two or three inches westward behind John Coles lento until it comes to the westward of said Coles back of ye chimley & four foot & a half further westward & so it runs south into the river. So far as ever said Lord had or ever ought to have had an interest in. *Signed:* Stephen Haskett; Elizabeth Haskett. Wife Elizabeth released dower. *Date:* 3 October 1671. *Witnesses:* Dorcas Veren; Hillard Veren Sr. *Acknowledged:* 6:8mo & Elizabeth yielded thirds. *Recorded:* 23:7mo:1680.

PHILLIP CROMWELL & EDMOND BRIDGES to WILLIAM SWEATLAND – (5:416) Phillip Cromwell (slaughterer) of Salem and Edmond Bridges (blacksmith) of Salem with consent of wife, Sarah, for consideration of 70 pounds to Phillip Cromwell sold to William Sweatland (tailer) of Salem dwelling house & shop & all ground belonging & adjoining containing about one quarter acre with all outhouses lying in Salem, late in tenure & occupation of Edmond Bridges & was lately bought in part from Thomas Flint and in part from Mr. John Ruck & is bounded with land late of Widdow Spooner now land of Mr. John Ruck north westerly & east northerly, ye land of Thomas Flint west southerly, and south easterly with street. *Signed:* Edmond R. Bridges [mark]; Phillip Cromwell; Sarah Bridges [mark]. *Date:* 18 September 1680. *Witnesses:*

John Cromwell; Isaac Williams. *Acknowledged:* 22, 7mo, 80. *Recorded:* 23:7mo:1680.

EBENEZER STOCKER to JOHN DOWLITTLE – (5:419) Ebenezer Stocker of Linn with consent of wife, for consideration of 200 pounds, sold to John Dowlittle of Boston messuage or tenement he lived in with all housing & lands thereto belonging lying in town of Linn bounded northerly by county road, westerly John Edmonds, southerly the marshes, easterly Noemans swamp, & also 9 acres of marshland lying below John Edmond's land. Provided if Ebenezer Stocker or heirs pay John Dowlittle or heirs 20 pounds current money yearly for eleven years from 31 August 1680 according to sevral bills obligatory being in number eleven then deed to be void. *Signed:* Ebenezer Stocker [mark]. *Date:* 31 August 1680. *Witnesses:* John Fuller; John Lewis. *Acknowledged:* 22 Sept 1680 by Ebenezer Stocker after John Dowlittle. *Recorded:* 23:7:1680. The above mortgage is fully satisfied & discharged forever. 14 booke folio 101.

JOHN DOWLITLE to EBENEZER STOCKER – (5:422) John Dowlittle (yeoman) of Rumney Marsh Suffox for divers good causes especially 240 pound in money sold to Ebenezer Stocker (husbandman) of Linn a parcell of land in Linn that John Dowlitle had purchased of Samuell Bennett of Rumney Marsh viz dwelling house & barn where Stocker now lives with all parcel of land where house stands bounded southerly with the several lots of Salt Marsh in Rumney Marsh, northerly with county highway, westerly with land of Capt. Marshall, John Diven & John Edmonds, & easterly ye town common usually called by the name of noemans swamp & all of the parcel & land & swamp as it is bounded & likewise 9 acres of salt marsh lying in ye first division of Rumney marsh, being bounded easterly with land of John Witt, westerly with land of Joseph Mansfield, northerly with land of John Edmonds, & southerly with lands of Allen Bread & William Merriman, where it is said all this parcel of upland & swamp is all except in or the highwayes into Rumney marsh is excepted that stand upon record. *Signed:* John Dowlettell. *Date:* 31 August 1680. *Witnesses:* John Lewis; John Fuller. *Acknowledged:* 22 Sept 1680. *Recorded:* 23:7mo:1680.

JONATHAN NEALE to SAMUELL SHATTOCK Jr – (5:425) Jonathan Neale (cordwinder) of Salem, son of John Neale deceased & heire to estate of Francis Lawes deceased with consent of Mary, now wife of Andrew Mansfield his honored mother & executrix of the will of Francis Lawes for consideration of 18 pounds sold to Samuell Shattock Jr (feltmaker) of Salem a certain parcel of land containing 20 poles belonging to the dwelling house Frances Lawes in his life time lived in; dementions of premises being viz: abutting or fronting against the street going from the meeting house to the town's end westward four poles in bredth & to run back into southward the same bredth of four poles, to make up the whole full 20 poles & is bounded northerly with the said street; easterly partly with a parcel that was John Porters deceased & partly with ground of John Cook & partly with land of William Lord senior, southerly with land of John Neale & westerly with land of Samuell Wakefield. *Signed:* Jonathan Neale; Mary Mansfield [mark]. *Date:* 16 Feb 1679. *Witnesses:* Hilliard Veren senior; William Lord Jr. *Acknowledged:* 25:6:1680 by both. *Recorded:* 4:9:1680.

LOTT KILLUM to JOSEPH POPE & BENJAMIN POPE – (5:429) Lott Killum (husbandman) of Salem with consent of wife, Hannah, for consideration of 3 pounds sold to Joseph Pope & Benjamin Pope of Salem a piece of fresh meadow lying in precincts & township of Salem 1 acre & a halfe being 12 poles & a halfe in bredth & twenty poles in length. It is bounded both easterly & westerly with land of Isaac Goodell & northerly upon meadow of Joseph & Benjamin Pope & southerly upon upland inclosed by Robert Goodell. *Signed:* Lott Killum; Hannah Killum [mark]. *Date:* 8 November 1680. *Witnesses:* John M. Upton; Richard Conrad. *Acknowledged:* 8 November 1680 & Hannah surrendered thirds. *Recorded:* 10:9:1680.

JOHN SAMPSON to DAVID PERKINS – (5:431) John Sampson (husbandman) of Beverly for consideration of two & twenty pounds sold to David Perkins (blacksmith) of Beverly half acre of land being an orchard, easterly bounded with Mr. Hale's land & the cow lane & southerly & westerly with land of David Perkins formerly Richard Haines land & 8 rod below great rock adjoining cow lane. *Signed:* John Sampson; Sarah Sampson [mark]. *Date:* 1 Nov 1680. *Witnesses:* William Hoare; Thomas Whitrig. *Acknowledged:* 2:9:1680 by John & Sarah wife & Sarah yielded thirds; land delivered by turfe & twig. *Recorded:* 10:9:1680.

ELLENOR STACYE to JOHN STACY – (5:433) Ellenor Stacye of Marblehead for consideration of 20 pounds which was granted to son John Stacye by order of ye county as for his portion sold to John Stacy one parcel of land being in Marblehead butting & bounded as follows: beginning at corner of Michael Coe's cow house or his mother's cow house, which is facing towards street towards Mrs Legg's cowhouse & from thence to go or range home cloase to a great white rock that is oppositt, against said John Stacy's dwelling house, & from said rock to go or joyne home with Michael Coe's ground or fence to the stone wall of his orchard, & along stone wall to lower end & from thence north east home to Thomas Pitman's stonewall fence & to range along said stonewall of Thomas Pitman's fence to a corner of said Pitman's wall that standeth out with a poynt near some plum trees, & over from thence to ye corner of Thomas Sowden's stone wale, wich may beare neere south & north one of another, & so along close by said wall home to said Stacy's house, & beyond his house to his stone wale where the rails are to the street & it was understood that after her death Ellenor gave John Stacy one cowes lease that lyeth in ye commons of Marblehead. *Signed:* Ellenor Stacy [mark]. *Date:* 16 November 1680. *Witnesses:* Thomas Dixy; Edw. Humphry Sr. *Acknowledged:* 16:9:1680. *Recorded:* 16:9:1680.

ELLENOR STACY to JOHN STACY & GRACE COES – (5:436)

Ellenor Stacy of Marblehead for divers good causes gave by deed of gift after her decease John Stacy son of John Stacy, her grandson and to Grace Coes daughter of Michaell Coes, her granddaughter a tract or parcel of land being in Marblehead being northwest from John Stacy's land, joyning close to his land lying & being between Thomas Pitman's land & Thomas Sowden's land & fronting to the street: the one half of that ground after her death to her grandchild John Stacy, & the other half after her death to her granddaughter Grace Coes and after her death the said tract of land to be equally divided between the two children as above said: to be parted in the middle on the street side. John Stacy to have northeast part next to Thomas Pitman's fence, & said Grace Coes to have the other part to Sowden's fence. If said John Stacy should die before he comes to age to possess his part then his part to his next brother, & if no brother then it falls in like manner to his sisters, and likewise if Grace Coes should die before she married or she comes to age it falls to her brother that is next, & if no brothers in like manner to her sister. But if Grace & her brothers & sisters none left to enjoy her part of the ground then her part to returned to said Stacy or his children. However said land not to be taken till Ellenor Stacy's death. After her death the parents of each child to take their equal parts until their children come of age & if any of children come to age then John Stacy son of John Stacy or any of his brothers or sisters come to age to injoy land then that part divided above said to goe to theire heires forever & likewise for the other part if Grace or any of her brothers or sisters comes of age to injoy that part & remaine to theire heires forever. *Signed:* Ellenor Stacy [mark]. *Date:* 16 Nov 1680. *Witnesses:* Thomas Dixy; Edw Humphrey Sr. *Acknowledged:* [no date]. *Recorded:* 16:9:1680.

ELLENOR STACY to MICHAEL COES & GRACE COES – (5:439)

Ellenor Stacy of Marblehead for divers consideration known to herself & a smale portion she promised daughter Grace by deed of gift deeded to son in law Michael Coes & daughter Grace Coes & their children who now or may be that is to say that Grace may have by Michael Coes her dwelling house in which she now lives & the ground it stands on, with cow lease belonging to said house & also a cow house that stands next the street facings Mr. Legg's house or cow house, & to have the ground from ye south west or west part of said Michael Coe's own house down along by the stone wale by Capt George Corwin's fence to the orchard, & also all her orchards & gardens & from westerly end of the cow house above said to goe right over to a rock that is opposite John Stacy's house, & so strait down to a stone wall of the orchard, all that ground up to his house. After her decease it is all to come into their possession, but as long as she lives & is able to keep in her possession only she has given and granted to her son & daughter abovesaid in her lifetime that they shall have the ground from the corner post of his medow next to her door, to run down to a pare tree that is in her orchard, just to Mr. Lattamore's fence & about four feet beyond the pare tree toward ye northward, as also the fruit of five or six trees that stands in there part of the orchard, & after her death all the house she now lives in with all the ground, cowhouse, cow lease, orchard garden & all above said is to be vallued by men what it may be worth, & if it doth amount to 45 pounds in money, then said Coes or heirs shall pay to her son Mark Stacy 5 pounds in money, but if it is valued at more than 45 pounds they shall not exceed the 5 pounds to her son Marke, if valued less than 45 pounds to give what is above the forty pounds to her son Mark Stacy. And if he be dead before then all to reman to said Coes & his wife Grace & to their children & heires forever. *Signed:* Ellenor Stacy [mark]. *Date:* 16 November 1680. *Witnesses:* Thomas Dixy; Edw Humphrey's. *Acknowledged:* 16:9:1680. *Recorded:* 16:9:1680.

WILLIAM DICKSEY to GEORGE STANLY – (5:442) William Dicksey of Beverly for consideration of 40 pounds sterling sold to George Stanly of Beverly 26 acres of land more or less lying in Beverly at the place called Bald Hill. The S. East bounds a smale ash, the S. West bounds a red oake the N West bounds a red oake, on the side of Bald Hill the noreast bounds a smale walnut, the land bounding on the south side of Thomas Patch's ground. *Signed:* William Dicksey [mark]; Anna Dicksie [mark]. *Release of dower:* wife does freely yield all her rights, title, dower & interest. *Date:* 8 January 1671. *Witnesses:* Joseph Gardner; Nathaniell Felton. *Acknowledged:* 8:11:72 & Anna, wife, yielded thirds. *Recorded:* 16:9:1680.

JOHN BROWNE to Mr. JOHN PILGRIM – (5:444) John Browne (marrenor) of Salem for valuable sum paid sold to Mr. John Pilgrim (marchant) of Salem certain parcel of ground containing 35 foot in breadth against ye south river at the barging point so called in Salem & to run ye same breadth backward so far as conveniently for the building of a warhouse, it being a town grant to said John Browne formerly fore a ware house, to have all interest in town grant, as it appears in the town records, provided said parcell having formerly granted by him to son James Browne deceased & since conveyed to John Marstone & by him conveyed to said John Pilgrim & there not appearing any legal instrument of conveyance of the same doe by these presents give assurance of same. *Signed:* John Browne. *Date:* 26 November 1680. *Witnesses:* Hillard Veren; Thomas Maule. *Acknowledged:* 27:9:1680. *Recorded:* 27:9:1680.

EZEKIELL FOGG – (5:446) Indenture made 20th day of March in 30th year of reign of Charles Second in the year 1677 between Ezekiell Fogg cittizen & skinner of London late of New England, merchant, of ye one part and Hezekiah Usher of Boston, merchant for & in behalf of Charles Gasfright of London, merchant, whose aturney he is, on ye other pt. witnesseth, yet whereas ye said Ezekiell Fogg standeth justly indebted to said Charles Gasfright, in the full & entire sum of one hundred thirty-eight pounds & five shillings & six pence half penny of New England money in which said sum being sued, he was condemned to pay the same by a court at Boston, together with 29 shillings six pence half penny, the cost of sute, the which being certified not to be performed, then ye said Ezekiell Fogg was again sued & cast in said sum at the general court of Assizes, held in New York on the 3rd day of October last past, with costs of that court also & as Ezekiell Fogg stands possest in his own right of ¼ part of a certain iron worke with 400 acres of land, together with eddifices, houses, & buildings lying between the towns of Linn & Redding being held by said Ezekiell Fogg together with Sir Richard Combs Knight, John Williams of Bristoll, merchant, & John Gifford of New England & several others in company which was known as the "silver worke," as by record of deeds in the town records of Salem, valued in England at 2000 pounds sterling, & is now in tenure of John Gifford on company's account for discharge of debt by Ezekiel Fogg by a special mortgage bound over & assigned unto Hezekiah Usher attorney unto Charles Gasfright ¼ of iron works, land, buildings, & ¼ part of stocks, profits, provided that if Ezekiell Fogg shall within space of 2 years after 20 March 1679 the sum of 138 pounds 5 shillings six pence half penny with costs in Boston then this mortgage shall be void but in case of failure of payment it shall be lawful for Hezekiah Usher on behalf of Charles Gasfright to dispose of ¼ of ironworkes till whole debt is discharged. *Signed:* Ezekiell Fogg. *Witnesses:* John Robson; John Juxson. Entered in the office of records att New York 22 of March 1677/8 in lib. & [?] B:fol57&Ct Matthias Nichols Secr. [on margin] Ezekiel Fogg acknowledged July 16:1678.

RICHARD KILLCUPP to RICHARD COOK & DANIELL HORNE –

(5:450) Richard Killcupp of Boston sold to Richard Cook & Daniell Horne, both of Boston, his house & lands in Charlestown with the comons & priviledges & 6 cowes & also 1/3 part of all mines & metals & wood upon land bought of Thomas Errington & 1/3 part of all works erected or to be erected on said ground, and 1/3 part of privilidges of the river & 16 acres of land according to the grant made by Thomas Errington dated 1:11mo:1649. Also assigns unto them the mortgage made by Thomas Errington 25:8mo:1650. Also house & yard in Boston bought of William Courser, upon condition if William Kilcupp shall pay or cause to be paid unto said Richard or Danill in the month of May 1652 the sum of 300 pounds sterling in moneys or marchantable wheat, barley, pease, beaver, or dry codfish at price current at the shop of Richard in Boston, that then this grant to be voyde. *Date:* 26:10mo:1650. *Acknowledged:* 27:10:1650. *Recorded:* foll:131 27:10m:1650.

True copy taken out of book of records. *Signature:* Edw. Ramson, Recorder. *Recorded:* 17:10mo:1680. *Signature:* Hilliard Veren, Recorder.

JOHN TAMLY to THOMAS MAULE – (5:451) Agreement dated 20

Nov 1680. Thomas Maule agree at his own cost to procure & set up a good substantial frame or building for a warehouse which shall contain 42 foot in length & between 20 & 22 foot in breadth & 10 foot stud, to be set up & completely finished as other warehouses ordinarily use to be, with a partition in the middle, & two doors at the cost & charge of Thomas Maule at or before the last day of May next ensuing date hereto which warehouse to be set up on Mr. John Tamly's wharf lying & being near his dwelling house in Salem & to be set on wharf as Mr. Maule & Mr. Tamly agree and if they not agree then two indifferent men shall judge. When it is set up & finished is to be equally betwixt them, Mr. Maule to have ½ & Mr. Tamly the other half. The house to be kept up in repair by Mr. Thomas Maule. Mr. John Tamly agree that Mr. Maule is to have free use of whole of Mr. John Tamly his wharfe in Salem soe farr as it shall not be prejudiciall to Mr. John Tamly: & Mr. Thomas Maule is to have to his use & not by Mr. John Tamly or any impowered by him hindered 21 foot in front to the water side, & some breath backward so far as the highway & Mr. John Tamly at his own cost is to keep the wharf in sufficient repair, neither to break covenant without mutual consent of other & if cannot agree either party to chose a man to end difference & bind ourselves each to other in sum of 50 pounds. *Signed:* Thomas Maule; John Tamly. *Date:* 26 Nov 1680. *Witnesses:* George Deane; Thomas Neale, Sr. *Acknowledged:* 26 Nov 1680. *Recorded:* 17:10:1680.

THOMAS PUTNAM & ISRAELL PORTER – (5:453) Whereas Leift. Thomas Putnam & Israell Porter being desired to appraize a parcel or parcels of land that was taken out from the farm late of Mr. James Allen of Boston which Frances Nurse of Salem purchased of him. Sd deponents swore they will appraize such to their best judgment taken upon oath. *Signed:* William Hathorne, assistant. *Date:* 15:1mo:1679:80. We whose names are above written and attested being showed two parcel of land by Francis Nurse of Salem, which he said were in his deed of sale of land bought of James Allen of Boston, bounded with a stake & rocks at one bound & a rotten tree roote at the other at the east end, & a maple tree & a brooke at the other end, or west end; & another slipe of land on the north side of farm, which the surveyor saith that ye land on ye south side is seventy & two acres, which land we judged worth thirty shilling per acre in money, & ye other slipe on ye other side of farm which the surveyor saith is two acres at twenty shillings an acre in money. Mr. Jonothan Danforth of Bilrike surveyer as he hath attested under his hand. *Signed:* Thomas Putnam; Israell Porter. The above written was brought by ye two appraizers, & owned by them to be their return, upon theire oath & accordingly recorded by me. *Signed:* Hilliard Veren, Recorded. *Recorded:* 17:10:1680.

EDWARD WOLLAN, senior to RICHARD SIMONS – (5:454) Edward Wollan, senior in consideration of 10 pounds 5 shillings sold to Richard Simons, (marrenor) of Salem parcel of 1/6 part of an acre in Salem part of his land lying behind southerly of his dwelling house & is in length east & west five poles & 6 foot, & in breadth north & south 5 poles wanting 13 inches or thereabouts, so much as to make the full 1/6 acre & is bounded easterly with land of William West, southerly & northerly with land of sd Edward Wollan, & westerly with highway left for the use of all the proprietors. Except said Simons is to leave out toward the lane or highway 7 foot in breadth through front of said parcel in part of highway unto which Edward Woollam can have by engaged for himself to leave out so much of his ground as to make it a convenient highway to pass & repass from the street with a cart, for the use of said Richard Simon together with the rest of the proprietors. *Signed:* Edward Wollan [mark]. *Date:* 28 October 1680. *Witnesses:* Hilliard Veren; Benjamin Marstone. *Acknowledged:* 28 October 1680. *Recorded:* 17:10:1680.

THOMAS BRACKETT to JOHN SMALE – (5:457) Thomas Brackett (planter) of Salem in consideration of 7 pounds sterling already paid, sold to John Smale (planter) of Salem a parcel of land containing 5 or 6 acres situated at north neck of the mouth of great cove belonging to Salem bounded with land of sd John Smale northerly & land of Nathaniel Felton southerly, land of Hugh Joanes westerly & abuts against water side easterly. *Signed:* Thomas Brackett: Alice Brackett. *Release of Dower:* Alice, wife of Thomas yielded her dower. *Date:* 14 May 1671. *Witnesses:* Nathaniel Felton; John Foster [mark]. *Acknowledged:* 20:10mo:1680 by witnesses. *Recorded:* 20:10:1680.

MOSES MAVERICK & EUNICE MAVERICK to WILLIAM HEWETT – (5:459) Moses Maverick (merchant) of Marblehead & his wife, Eunice, for consideration of 150 pounds of lawful money of New England sold to William Hewett (fisherman) of Marblehead all that thine messuage & tenement lying & being in Marblehead along with all land belonging to same containing by estimation 40 acres & lately in the tenure of Phillip Welch bounded on northeast side by land of Nathaniel Walton & on southwest by land of John Deverix & on northwest by ye comon & on southwest by the harbor & also two cowes comonages being within township of Marblehead & upon said common together with all houses, edifices, buildings, fences, trees. *Signed:* Moses Maverick; Eunice Maverick. *Date:* 7 October 1679. *Witnesses:* Samuel Cheever; Thomas Cheever. *Acknowledged:* 16 June 1680 by both. *Recorded:* 20:10:1680.

MARY CROMWELL to ROBERT SOLLAS – (5:462) Mary Cromwell, wife of Phillip Cromwell & administratrix of Robert Lemon former husband deceased for good considerations & natural affection to Robert Sollas the son of her daughter Grace Sollas deceased, granted to Robert Sollas ½ of her dwelling house & grounds on which it stands & ½ of orchards & all ground adjoining ½ thereof the whole ground & being about ½ acre that is westerly end of house which was her former husband's Robert Lemon's which he dwelled in in his lifetime. The said westerly end containing one lower & one upper room & a seller under it with the chimley to that end belonging & halfe sd halfe acre thereto belonging, viz: the westerly side being equally divided from the south end next ye water side. Through the ground to the north end thereof which said house & grounds as it lyes now together is lying in Salem & bounded southerly against south harbour, westerly by land of William Dicer, northerly by land of Andrew Woodbery & westerly by land now or lately by land of Mathew Nixon. *Signed:* Mary Cromwell [mark]. *Date:* 21 October 1680. *Witnesses:* Mary Mackmallen [mark]; Hilliard Veren, secr. *Acknowledged:* 3rd 9mo. *Recorded:* 20:10:1680.

JEREMIAH BELCHER, SR to JAMES POWLEY/POWLEN – (5:465) Jeremiah Belcher, Sr. of Ipswich sold to James Powlen/Powley (gunsmith) of Salem with consent of wife, Mary, for consideration of 11 pounds, a certain parcel of upland & meadow two hundred acres situated on the northern side of the Merrimack River in the county of Essex 100 poles in bredth fronting on the Merimack river, to the south 320 poles in length ranging on his own land easterly, northerly on land he had given to his son-in-law Joseph Russell, westerly on land which he sold to Joseph Hardy bodering on the common land, intent being 100 poles in breadth fronting upon said river, the eastern side of land running back northerly 320 poles butting on his own land to a tree marked BP, on ye western side 320 poles ranging on land which he sold to Joseph Hardy junior to a tree marked PH standing near ye river. And also to make good & sure to said Powland as much meadow as shall make up 20 acres within halfe a mile distant from bargained premises in case there be not soe much found in said content of two hundred acres. *Signed:* Jeremiah Belcher; Mary Belcher [her mark]. *Date:* 13 July 1680. *Witnesses:* Joseph Hardy, Jr.; Richard Croade. *Acknowledged:* 13 July 1680 by both. *Recorded:* 20:10:1680.

JOSIAH WHITE to RESOLVED WHITE – (5:468) Josiah White for divers good causes & 20 pounds current money paid & secured to be paid & more especially that childlike affection & good will he have & beare sold to his father, Resolved White all his rights title & interest in ye within, mentioned, given & granted parcel of land without hinderance from him or heirs... or Remember his wife. *Signed:* Josiah White. *Date:* 30 December 1680. *Witnesses:* Samuell Archard; Hilliard Veren. *Acknowledged:* 30 December 1680. *Recorded:* 31:10:1680.
Above assignment indorsed on back side of deed of gift made by Resolved White to Josiah White & is recorded book 4th foll:177 the 15:11:1677. *Signed:* Hilliard Veren Recorder.

RESOLVED WHITE to JOHN HATHORNE – (5:470) Resolved White of Salem for consideration of 60 pounds current money, (wife Abigail yielded dower) sold to John Hathorne (merchant) of Salem certain parcel of land containing fourer acres & 10 poles as it was bounded out by the Marshall & possessing given Resolved White by virtue of an execution levied upon same, to satisfy a judgment of account against Nicholas Manning, as by the records of the Salem Court may appeere in Salem bounded easterly by land of Jonathan Pickering, southerly with ye milne pond, westerly partly by land of Nicholas Manning & partly by land of John Pickering, & northerly by highway. *Signed:* Resolved White: Abigail White [mark]. *Date:* 31 December 1680. *Witnesses:* Hilliard Veren; Benjamin Marstone; William Dounton. *Acknowledged:* 31 December 1680 by both. *Recorded:* 31:10:1680.

MARY DARLING to THOMAS MAULE – (5:473) Mary Darling of Salem, daughter of John Darling, with consent of her father John Darling, administrator of her grandfather Richard Bishop deceased and also with consent of her mother Mary Darling, for consideration of a valuable sum of of money in hand paid, sold to Thomas Maule of Salem a small tract of land in Salem adjoining land of father John Darling in quantity of half an acre viz; fourer score poles which was given Mary Darling by deceased grandfather by will bounded easterly with land of Mr. Croade, northerly with land of Thomas Bishop, in ye possession of Thomas Robbins, westerly with land that was formerly Widdow Spooners, southerly with land of father John Darling & Roger Darbie. *Signed:* Mary Darling [mark]; John Darling [mark]. *Date:* 19 Nov 1680. *Witnesses:* George Deane; Frances Neale senr. *Acknowledged:* 9 Nov 1680 by John; 29 Nov 1680 by Mary. *Recorded:* 5:11:1680.

Endorsed on back side of original bill Benjamin Fuller, Mary's husband consenting because here was not roome to record it, it is recorded in 6th book foll:63 & belongs to this deed.

JEREMIAH NEALE & PETER CHEEVERS – (5:476) Under written being chosen by Jeremiah Neale & Peter Cheevers to make a division between them of piece of salt marsh about ½ acre & a parcel of about 9 acres of upland lately purchased by Neale & Cheevers in joint partnership they have equally disburstin of said purchase: allotted to disburstin Jeremiah Neale for his part of upland the west side of lot, 8 poles in breadth at south end, & at northerly end four poles in bredth, to run straight from bound to bound on east side, & west on said Neale's land, & meadow that lies along side of it, and above said Cheevers to have all the rest of upland within the bounds of that lot that lies on the east side of afore said east side of straight line. The saltmarsh being divided & bounded by two stakes, they allot unto Neale for his part the northerly of it, & Cheevers to have the rest of it up to the highway over the brook. The said Neale & Cheevers to allow each other convenient highways for carting as occasion may require & each of them have privilege for taking & using stones or rockes upon either part. Underwtitten accept within mentioned division. *Signed:* Jeremiah Neale; Peeter Cheevers. *Date:* 24 March 1679:80. *Witnesses:* Bartho. Gedney; John Pickering; Frances Skerry. *Acknowledged:* 22:November:80. *Recorded:* 8:11:1680.

ABRAHAM COLE to JOSEPH SWASY – (5:477) Abraham Cole (taylor) of Salem with wife Sarah signing in consent, for consideration of 40 pounds in silver sold to Joseph Swasy (marrenor) of Salem dwelling house in Salem now in tenure & possession of wife of Thomas Parnell together with land thereto belonging as it is now fenced in being butted southerly on his own land, westerly by street, easterly by land of Edward Gaskill one part, & land of Joshua Buffum ye other part that is for the addition of the two lengths of railes in bredth which he has by these presents sold unto Joseph Swazy on the back side of his house northerly, & bredth of ye said two lengths of railes, as now marked & agreed upon to run exactly upon a square, ranging upon his own lands northerly, upon a true & faithfull intent & meaning, unto ye land of Joshua Buffam as foresaid easterly. *Signed:* Abraham Cole; Sara Cole. *Date:* 9 August 1680. *Witnesses:* Thomas Ruck; Richard Croade. *Acknowledged:* 26 August 1680. *Recorded:* 14 January 1680. Delivered by turfe & twigg in presence of John Coake & Samuell Sibley.

JOHN DARLAND to ROGER DERBY – (5:480) John Darland (seaman) of Salem with wife Mary signing in consent, for consideration of 27 pounds in silver sold to Roger Derby (chandler) of Ipswich all his piece of ground to the western side of his dwelling house in Salem 5 poles & a half in length to the streetward, & two poles & ½ backward to the land now in the tenure of Thomas Robbins bounded upon land of John Ruck & John Simpson westerly upon towne streete sotherly upon land that was Richard Bishop in tennour of Thomas Robbins northerly as fence stands to dwelling house & ground of said John Darland easterly running square from said Darlands house out to streete only said Darland to have liberty upon necessary ocasions for mending of said Darlands house to come upon land of said Derby. *Signed:* John Darland [mark]; Mary Darland [mark]. *Date:* 8 February 1678/79. *Witnesses:* Thomas Robbins; Richard Croade. *Acknowledged:* by both – no date. *Recorded:* 27 January 1680.

HILLIARD VEREN Jun'r to WILLIAM BROWNE Jun'r – (5:483) Hilliard Veren Jun'r of Salem for consideration of a valuable sume sold to William Browne Jun'r (merchant) of Salem parcel of land Salem 18 feet both in front & reare & that bredth through bredth of the land bounded with land of Captain William Browne Jun'r east land of Geo. Keaser south the lane west & Hilliard Veren Jun'r to north & Hilliard Veren obleiges himself to make & maintaine upon his proper charge the whole of the end fence to the south of his ground provided he have a benefit of 18 foot of ground sold as above for a lane or highway to south part of his ground. *Signed:* Hilliard Veren Jun'r. *Date:* 8 November 1679. *Witnesses:* Nehemiah Willoughby; Charles Redford with seizin & possession given of premises by turfe & twigg. *Acknowledged:* 27 January 1680 by Mr. Willoughby & Charles Redford. *Recorded:* 27 January 1680.

JOSIAH HASCALL to THOMAS GAGE – (5:485) Josiah Hascall of Gloster for consideration of 2 pounds sterling sold to Thomas Gage (smith) of Beverly quarter acre of land in towne of Beverly bounded westerly by highway southerly by land of John Bennett northerly & easterly by land of said Josiah Hascall being 3 pole wide to highway & at other end alsoe. *Signed:* Josiah Hascall. *Date:* 22 September 1680. *Witnesses:* Samuell Hardie; Roger Hascall. *Acknowledged:* 21 September 1680. *Recorded:* 27 January 1680.

GEORGE DEANE – THOMAS DEANE – WILLIAM LONGSTAFFS – (5:487) Testimoneys of George Deane aged about 40 yeares & his son Thomas Deane aged about 16 yeares & William Longstaffs aged about 50 yeares: all above written doe testifie that on the 21 day of the eleventh month in yeare 1680 they heard Thomas Maule say unto Richard Croade, "why doth thy wife say my new house stands two foot on thy land," then Richard Croade made this answer to Tho. Maule, that it was but womans talk, & he could not help it, there talke, "for," saith Richard Croade, "I sett downe ye fences betweene my neighbour Maule and me, & I sett it in the same places where it stand always before, & my neighbour Maule & I did agree very lovingly about it till wee come to the back of the oven neere the streete, which went about two foot further than the outside of his new house now stands, & what words then passed between me & my neighbor Maule about the oven were not worth the minding, for it was not all that wee then contended about worth a farthing. Soe when I had sett down the fences, my neighbour Maule & I divided it equally betweene us & my neighbor Maule paid me for my labor, & after this was all done I made Thomas Maule's bill of sale, which runs as now bounded & fenced in & alsoe I become a witnes to the bill of sale." And to the truth heareof George Deane, Thomas Deane and William Longstaff set our hands. *Date:* 21:11mo:1680.

George Deane & Thomas Deane swore to truth of above written 24:11mo:1680. *Signed:* Bartholmew Gedney Assist. This testimony referrs to bill of sale of George Deane to sd Maule recorded in 4th book foll:98.

GEORGE KEASER to JOHN CROMWELL – (5:488) George Keaser (tanner) of Salem for consideration of 15 pounds sterling sold to John Cromwell (slautherer) of Salem that parcel he bought of Christopher Waller in length 8 pole & in bredth 2 pole & 12 foot in Salem bounded with som land of Mathew Price on north land of James Brown (glazier) on south som land of Joseph Miles on east & with lane or highwaye west. *Signed:* George Keaser. *Date:* 28 May 1674. *Witnesses:* Sara Parkman; Hilliard Veren senr. *Acknowledged:* 1 February 1680. *Recorded:* 5:12:1680.

MATHEW NIXON & WALTER & BRIDGETT WHITFORD – (5:490) Indenture made 16 December 1678 between Mathew Nixon of Salem (fisherman) of one part & Walter Whitford of Salem (fisherman) & Bridgett his wife of other part: Mathew Nixon for divers good causes &

considerations especially for & in consideration that Walter Whitford & Bridgett or either of theire providing for & comfortably maintaining or causing to be maintained by them sd Mathew Nixon the remaining part of his naturall life well & sufficiently with meate, drink & apparel, washing & lodging & all other necessaryes as well in sickness as in helth doe grant & confirm sd Walter Whitford & Bridgett his wife my dwelling house with all land adjoining containing the orchard garden & yard between 50 & 60 pole of ground in Salem bounded by ground of Thomas Seale sotherly excepting a waye to go out to ye waterside on east side of sd Searles: & upon east side backward by a strip of orchard of sd Thomas Searles, & north by land of Andrew Woodberry & westerly by land of Charles Knights. Also all & singular my other estate moveables & immoveables, household goods, chattels proprieties, privilidges, implements & comodyties of what kind & nature soever be found & have put sd Walter & Bridgett his wife into peaceable possession of all premises by delivery of 12 pence which I have paid unto them the day & date of these presents: & sd Walter Whitford & Bridgett wife in consideration of bargained premises promise & ingaged ourselves to provide for & well & comfortably mainetaine with all things necessary for this life sd Mathew Nixon or cause him to be maintained during terme of his naturall life. *Signed:* Mathew Nixon [mark]; Walter Whitford; Bridgett Whitford [mark]. *Date:* day first above written. *Witness:* Bridged Webb [mark]. *Acknowledged:* 7 February 1680 by all 3. *Recorded:* 7:12mo:1680.

JOHN RUCK sen'r to PHILLIP CROMWELL – (5:493) John Ruck sen'r (marchant) in county of Essex for consideration of 50 shillings sold to Phillip Cromwell (slautherer) of Salem a strip of upland in field called south field appertaining to Salem & which strip was formerly land of his father in law Thomas Spooner ½ acre bounded: on land of sd John Ruck eastsotherly upon towne common southwesterly to smale white wood tree standing neere fence mark & on both sides upon marsh of Mr. Phillip Cromwell northeasterly. *Signed:* John Ruck; Elizabeth Ruck. *Date:* 29 Aprill 1680. *Witnesses:* Thomas Ruck; Abigall Ruck. *Acknowledged:* 14:3mo:80. *Recorded:* 9:12mo:1680.

RICHARD BRACKENBURY – (5:495) Richard Brackenbury of Beverly aged 80 years testifieth that he came to New England with John Endecott Esq. late Govenor of New England deceased & that we came ashore at place now called Salem 6th of September 1628 52 yeares ago: at Salem wee found liveing old Goodman Norman & his sons, William Allen & Walter Knight & others: those owned that they came over upon the accot of a company of England called by us by the name of Dorchester company for Dorchester marchants: they had sundry houses built at Salem, as alsoe John

Woodbery, Mr. Conant, Peeter Palfery, John Balch & others & they declared yt they had an house built at Cape An for ye Dorchester company: & I having waited upon Mr. Endecott when he attended the company of Massachusetts pattenties, when they kept theire Court in Comewell Street in London I understood that this company of London having bought out ye right of the Dorchester marchants in New England & that Mr. Endecott had power to take possession of theire right in New England which Mr. Endecott did & in particular of an house built at Cape Ann which Walter Knight & the rest said they built for Dorchester men & soe I was sent with them to Cape Ann to pull downe ye sd house for Mr. Endecotts use, the which wee did: the same yeare we came over: according to my best remembrance, it was that we took a further possession on ye north side of Salem ferry called Cape Ann side: by cutting thach for our houses & soon after laid out lots for our tillage land on ye sd Cape An side & quickly after sundry houses were built on ye Cape Ann side & I myself have lived there now for about 40 yeares & I with sundry others have been subdueing the wilderness & improving the feilds & comons there, as a part of Salem, while we belonged to it, & since as inhabitants of Beverly for these 50 yeares, & never yt I heard of disturbed in our possessions, either by the Indians or others, save in our late unhappy war with the heathen, neither have I heard by myselfe, or any other inhabitants with us, for the space of these 50 yeares, yt Mr. Mason or any, by, from or under him did take any possession or lay any claime to any lands heare, save now in his last claim within this yeare or two.

Richard Brackenbury made oath to truth of above written 20th day of January 1680 before Bartholmew Gedney, Assistant, in the Colloney of Massachusetts. *Recorded:* 16:12mo:1680.

WILLIAM DIXY – (5:497)   William Dixy of Beverly aged about 73 yeares testifieth: that I came to New England & arrived in June 1629 at Cape An where wee found the signes of buildings & plantation work & saw no English people, soe we sailed to the place now called Salem, where we found Mr. John Endecot, Govenor, & sundry inhabitants besides some of whom said they had beene servants to Dorchester company & had built at Cape Ann sundry yeares before wee came over: when we came to dwell here the Indians bid us welcome & showed themselves very glad that we came to dwell among them & I understood they had kindly entertained the English that came hether before wee came & the English & the Indians had a feild in comon fenced in together & the Indians fled to shelter themselves under the English oft times saying they were afraid of theire enemy Indians in the contry in particular I remember sometime after wee arrived the Agawam Indians complained to Mr. Endicott that they were afraid of other

Indians called as I take it Tawateens: Hugh Browne was sent with others in a boat to Agawam for the Indianes reliefe & at other times we gave our neighbour Indians protection from the enemy Indians. Taken upon oath 16 February 1680 before William Browne & Bartholmew Gedney Assistants. *Recorded:* 16:12:1680.

HUMPHRY WOODBERY – (5:498) Humphry Woodbery of Beverly aged about 72 yeares testifieth: that when I lived in Sumersetsheire in England I remember that my father John Woodberye (since deceased) did about 56 yeares agoe remove for New England, & I then traveled with him as farr as Dorchester, & I understood that my said father came to New England by order of a company caled Dorchester company (among whome Mr. White of Dorchester in England was an active instrument) & that my father & the company with him, brought cattle & other things to Cape Ann for plantation work & theire built an house & kept theire cattle, & sett up fishing, & afterwards some of them removed to a neck of land since caled Salem: after about 3 yeares absence my sd father returned to England, & made us acquainted with what setlement they had made in New England & that he was sent back by some that intended to setle a plantation about 3 leagues west of Cape Ann to further this designe, after about halfe a yeares stay in England, my father returned to New England & brought me with him, we arived at the place now caled Salem in or about the month of June 1628, where we found severall persons that said they were servants to ye Dorchester company, & I had built another house for them at Salem besides that at Cape Ann: the latter of that sumer 1628 John Endecot Esqr: came over, Governor, declaring his power from a company of pattentees in or about London, & that they had bought the houses, boates & servants which belonged to ye Dorchester company & that ye said Endecott had power to receive them which accordingly he did take possession of: when we setled, the Indians never then molested us, in our improvements or sitting downe, either in Salem or Beverly sides of the ferry, but shewed themselves very glad of our company, & came and planted by us & often times came to us for shelter, saying they were afraid of theire enemy Indians up in the contry, & wee did shelter them when they fled to us, & wee had theire free leave to build & plant where we have taken up lands, the same yeare or the next after we came to Salem wee cutt hay for the cattle wee brought over on ye side of the ferry now caled Beverly, & I have kept our psossession their ever since by cutting hay or thatch or timber & boards, & by laying out lotts for tillage, & then by peoples planting: & some time after building & dwelling heere, where I with others have lived about 40 yeares: in all this time of my being in New England, I have never heard that Mr. Mason tooke possession heare, disbursed estate upon, or laid any claime to this place of oures, save the discourses of a claime within this yeare or two.

The testimony within taken upon oath 16:February 1680 before William Browne & Bartholmew Gedney, Assistants. *Recorded:* 16:12mo:1680.

THOMAS ROBBINS to PHILLIP CROMWELL – (5:500) Thomas Robbins (carpenter) of Salem for consideration of 6 pounds 8 sh. in pay long since received sold to Phillip Cromwell (slautherer) of Salem a piece of land in Salem as fenced in 2 acres bounded: on the comon lane towards Bass river ferry sotherly, easterly by lane ranging towards said ferry, upon the front against the north river, bounding upon the comon roade going towards the ferry, aforesd ags't the north river, westerly on land of Jeffery Massy in possession of John Massey. *Signed:* Thomas Robbins. *Date:* 18 Aprill 1680. *Witnesses:* John Massy; Richard Croade. *Acknowledged:* 19:2mo:1680. *Recorded:* 21:12mo:1680.

ANNA ROOTEN to HUGH ALLEY – (5:503) Anna Rooten widow and relict of Richard Rooten, late of Linn, husbandman deceased, in consideration of love and affection she bore well beloved friend Hugh Alley, who lived with her several years, and also divers other good causes and especially that Hugh Alley had undertaken to maintain her during her natural life as by bond bearing date of these presents gave Hugh Alley all her housing lands meadow or marsh ground with all gardens, orchards within township of Linn. *Signed:* Ann Rooten [mark]. *Date:* 20 December 1680. *Witnesses:* Samuell Johnson; Daniell Johnson. *Acknowledged:* March 5:1680:1 Anna Rooten and witnesses. *Recorded:* 15:2mo:1680.

ABRAHAM COLE to TOWNE of SALEM – (5:505) Abraham Cole of Salem, taylor, having mortgaged his dwelling house for payment of 196 pounds 8 shillings and 7 pence for which he stood indebted to town of Salem upon balance of accounts and being constable and there being paid since by the order of Selectmen of Salem in part of said sum 98 pounds 7 shillings and 5 pence and there being yet due 98 pounds 1 shilling 2 pence and the former mortgage being null and void, in consideration of said collateral sum of 98 pounds 1 shilling 2 pence still remaining due to towne of Salem, sold to Selectmen of Salem in behalf of the towne and for said town's use all his dwelling house with shop and all appurtenances with ground thereto belonging being all within fence on north side of said house being parted from ground or yard belonging to the old house by a fence a little distance to the southward of the old house which said house and ground now sold is bounded with the broad street southerly the lane westerly the said old house and ground lately his now Jo: Swasy's northerly, the land of Edward Gaskin easterly, provided if Abraham Cole pay the Selectmen of town of Salem the sum of 98 pounds 1 shilling and 2 pence at or before 25 day of March 1682 in pay according as the rates in that yeare he was constable was to be paid or sooner if the county treasurer do require it of towne then to be paid, if not, then at said 25th of March aforesaid, which payment being made the sale to be void, provided if said house and ground shall be seized for want of payment and sold for more than the sum of 98 pounds 1 shilling 2 pence with just damages, the overplus to be repaid to said Abraham Cole. *Signed:* Abraham Cole. *Date:* 28 February 1680. *Witnesses:* Wm. Browne Junior; Jonathan Corwin; John Corwin; John Hathorne. *Acknowledged:* 11th of March 1680:1. *Recorded:* 16:March:1680:1.

NATHANIEL FELTON to JOHN FREIND – (5:508) Nathaniel Felton of Salem in consideration of 4 pounds in hand paid sold to Jon. Freind of Salem 20 acres of land next to land of John Bacheler formerly of John Scudder and on the comon upon Ryall's side. *Signed:* Nathaniell Felton. *Date:* 7th of 18th[sic] month 1658. *Witnesses:* Phillip Cromwell; John Gedney. *Acknowledged:* 7:10mo:58. *Recorded:* 28:March:1681.

SAMUELL FREIND to LAURANCE LEACH – (5:509) Samuell Freind of Manchester gave bill witnessing that he had sold to Laurance Leach of Salem now deceased the mill and mill house standing in Bass river with all appurtenances together with 2 acres of land adjoining and 20 acres a little distance of all on Royalls neck side and there being no bill of sale made he confirmed sale to John Leach son to Laurance Leach aforesaid and bound himself to making good thereof. *Signed:* Samuel Freind. *Date:* 7:7mo:65. *Witnesses:* Roger Conant; William Walton. *Acknowledged:* 28th March 1681. *Recorded:* 28 March 1681. The 15:March:81: Samuell Freind acknowledged he subscribed this bill of sale and took pay for land. *Witnesses:* Zachariah Herick; Phillip Fowler.

JOHN GOLD to JOSEPH ESTY – (5:510) John Gold (husbandman) of Topsfeild with consent of wife Sarah in consideration of 40 pounds in hand paid by bills sold Joseph Esty (weaver) of Topsfeild parcel of upland and swamp, 30 acres, within bounds of Topsfeild at red oak by land of said Gold running east as trees are marked to white oak then running south or southeast to red oak standing upon the brow of hill called Bellingate and from that tree west or southwest down to heap of stones by Samuell Stanlies fence, running along by said Stanlyes fence north or northeast up to tree first mentioned bounded on every side with land of aforesaid Gold and Samuell Stanlies land. John Gold granted to Joseph Esty liberty that he had in farmer Stanlyes fence by Joseph Estys land as appeared by deed under Mathew Stanly's hand which was to be maintained, a sufficient 5 raile fence, and also granted a way to Joseph Esty to come from his land all along by Samuell Stanlies fence to the said Goold his way by Mathew

Stanly's land and as the highway ran or over the foard by said Stanlyes so he may doe as little damage to said Stanly as he could and also Joseph Esty had liberty to come over said Goolds land toward Topsfeild to come to mill and meeting said Esty always in time of the year set up fences of Goold as he is to come through or pull down to go in or out at, Esty also had liberty to drive his cattle to the comon over said Goold's land and if Goold fenced in his land so as he cannot come to the common, with going throu the said Goolds fence. *Signed:* John Goold, sen'r; Sarah Goold. *Date:* 17 December 1680. *Witnesses:* John How; Isaack Esty, sen'r. *Acknowledged:* 11th March 1680. *Recorded:* 30 March 1681.

SAMUELL PRINCE to JOHN RUCK – (5:513) Samuell Prince (taylor) of Salem in consideration of 5 pounds 5 shillings sold to John Ruck, sen'r (merchant) of Salem parcel of salt marsh or meadow ground, ½ acre and ½ of ¼ acre which was bequeathed to him by will of his father Richard Prince deceased situated in bounds of Salem on south side of said towne near southfeild and bounded with some marsh formerly of Thomas Browning's deceased to south, and some marsh formerly of William Flint's deceased north, upland formerly of Elias Stileman east and some land formerly of widow Spooner's west. *Signed:* Samuell Prince. *Date:* 21 March 1680:81. *Witnesses:* William Dounton; Hilliard Veren. *Acknowledged:* 21 March 1680:81. *Recorded:* 30:March:1681.

JOHN NORMAN to ROB'T KNIGHTS – (5:515) John Norman of Manchester for valuable consideration sold to Rob't Knights of Marblehead parcel of land near the meeting house of Marblehead that was formerly fenced in by John Peach and formerly belonged to said John Peach, Jun'r and bought by John Norman. *Signed:* John Norman. *Date:* 28:September:1651. *Witnesses:* Frances Johnson; Edward Wharton. *Acknowledged:* by witness 22 February 1680. *Recorded:* 5 April:1681.

WILLIAM LORD to ELEAZER GILES – (5:516) William Lord (planter) of Salem in consideration of 12 pounds 12 shillings sold to Eleazer Giles (husbandman) of same towne parcel of meadow, 2 acres, in limits of Salem and in farm of Samuell Verry by Leader pond being 2 acres excepted and reserved out of said farm formerly by Mr. Phillip Veren and at the north end of greate meddow on westward side of brook that runs down through meadow and is bounded northerly and westerly with upland of said Samuel Verry, easterly with brook, and sotherly with meadow of said Verry. *Signed:* William Lord. *Witnesses:* Hillard Veren sen'r; Henry Coleburne. *Acknowledged:* no date. *Recorded:* 1:Apr 1681.

JOSHUA REA to JEREMIAH WATTS – (5:517) Joseph Rea (yeoman) of Salem in consideration of 10 pounds sold to Jeremiah Watts (dish turner) of same towne parcel of land 10 acres being part of ground belonging to his farme where he lived & a part of land lately bought of town of Salem bounded easterly partly with land of Edward Bishop & corner bound is walnut tree & partly on the easter side with some land of Joseph Herrick & sotherly with contry roade where at corner bounds is smale oak tree marked next ye roade westerly & northerly bounded with his own land where two northerly bounds is at the corners a heape of stones laid about a stake at each corner. *Signed:* Joshua Rea. *Date:* 18 March 1677:8. *Witnesses:* John Hathorne; Israell Porter. *Acknowledged:* 21:2mo:1680. *Recorded:* 6:2mo:1681.

SAMUELL BRABROOK to JEREMIAH WATTS – (5:520) Samuell Brabrook in consideration of 50 shillings in silver and a cotton rug about 40 shillings price sold to his father in law Jeremiah Watts the acre of land which he bought of father in law Jeremiah Watts which is joining to Edward Bishop's land eastward and southward to contry roade & upward joining to said Jeremiah Watt's own land. *Signed:* Samuell Brabrook; Mary Brabrook [mark]. *Date:* 19 March 1680. *Witnesses:* Edward Bishop; Joseph Herrick. *Acknowledged:* 6 Aprill 1681. *Recorded:* 6:2mo:1681. *Dower:* Mary delivered up right of dower.

JOHN GEDNEY Sen'r to SAMUELL SHATTOCK Sen'r – (5:521) John Gedney Sen'r (vintner) of Salem for consideration of 2 pounds 10 shillings sold to Samuell Shattock Sen'r (felt maker) of same place his part of a warehouse that he held in part ownership with Mr. Samuell Gardner sen'r, his part being that end from the partition to north which said warehouse stands at east side of cove neere land of Nathaniell Pickman & is over against Mr. Elias Stilemans warehouse that stands on westerne side of said cove alsoe all his right in ground said north end of said warehouse stands upon. *Signed:* John Gedney [mark]. *Date:* 11 Aprill 1681. *Witnesses:* Nathaniell Beadle; Susanah Gedney. *Acknowledged:* 11:April:81. *Recorded:* 14:2mo:1681.

THOMAS ROBBINS to WILLIAM PINSON & REBECKA PINSON – (5:523) Thomas Robbins of Salem in consideration of naturall affection he bore kinsman William Pinson & his wife Rebecka (who is his sister's daughter) as other good causes more especially that said William Pinson hath engaged himself as by bond bearing date of these presents will appeere well & sufficiently to provide for him and his wife Mary both in sickness & in health during his naturall life, gave all his good chattels lands housing cattell money plate dues debts rings household stuff brass pewter & all other substance whatsoever moveable & immoveable quick & dead of what kind & nature soever condition or quallity soever same may be either in his custody & possession of any other person excepting what he has already disposed of by will bearing date of these presents the true meaning of. Above is to invest William Pinson in continued possession of premises conditionally that he doe & performe as his executor what is contained in his will already made & signed before above instrument which will beare date of these presents. *Signed:* Thomas Robbins [mark]. *Date:* 18 Aprill 1681. *Witnesses:* Frances Neal sen'r; George Thomas. *Acknowledged:* 18 Aprill 1681. *Recorded:* 19:Aprill:81.

JOHN PUTNAM to Capt. THOMAS LOTHROP – (5:525) John Putnam (yeoman) of Salem for valuable consideration sold to Capt. Thomas Lothrop of aforesaid towne 2 parcels of land 60 acres, one being all his part of meddow that was Major Hathornes formerly containing the eight part of the greate meddow, the other part adjoining to land of Thomas Puttnam on the west, land of John Ruck on north, land of John Putnam on east & land of Thomas Putnam on south, all lands being in township of Salem. *Signed:* John Putnam. *Date:* 22 June 1669. *Witnesses:* William Dounton; Thomas Putnam. *Acknowledged:* 30:4:69. *Recorded:* 26:2mo:1681.

GEORGE PIKE to AMBROSE GALE – (5:527) George Pike (fisherman) of Marblehead in consideration of 48 pounds & in security of paiment of above said sume to Ambrose Gale of same place deeded all his housing and land whereon same stood, ¼ acre in Marblehead adjoyning house and land of Samuell Condy & fronting to the waye side alsoe moyety of halfe of my catch formerly knowne by name of "The Brothers' Adventure" together with all furniture tackling & apparel whatsoever to the said moyety belonging & bought formerly of Mr. John Freeman provided if George Pike pay or cause to be paid 48 pounds at or before last of September next come twelve mo. which will be 1675 without any cover, fraude or deceite paying some part at the end of every fishing season that whole debt may be discharged in moneye at or before abovesaid time deed shall be voyde. *Signed:* George Pike [mark]. *Date:* 1 August 1674. *Witnesses:* Moses Maverick; Samuell Ward. *Acknowledged:* 9 May 1681. *Recorded:* 9 May 1681.

(5:529) **ESSEX REGISTRY OF DEEDS SOUTHERN DISTRICT SALEM MASS.** OCT° 8, 1875
The foregoing copy of the Fifth Book of Records of Deeds for Salem and vicinity was made in 1855 under the direction of the County

Commissioners. It has now been examined and corrected and is a true copy of the original.

Attest, Ephm. Brown Reg:

INDEX

BENET/BENETT/
  BENNET/BENNETT
John, 9, 14, 15, 23, 51-53, 59, 60, 77
Henry, 5
Samuell, 34, 67
BERRY
Edward, 22
BERTAUTE
Jean, 29
BILES
Eliza (___), 38
Elizabeth (___), 38
Jonathan, 38
BISHOP
___, Mr., 28
Edward, 85
Richard, 21, 76, 77
Thomas, 76
BLANO
___, Mr., 38, 39
BLEVIN
John, 42
BLINDMAN
Richard, 25
BLY
John, 40
BONDS
Edward, 26
BOOTEMAN
Jeremiah, 41
BOOTHE
George, 30
BOSWORTH
Hanill, 4
BOWDITCH
William, 48
BOYCE
John, 64
Joseph, 64
BRABROOK
Mary, 85
Samuell, 85
BRACKENBUR
Richard, 79, 80
BRACKETT
Alice (___), 74
Peeter, 57
Thomas, 18, 19, 73, 74
BRATTLE
Thomas, 34

BRAYBROOK
Richard, 36, 37
BREAD/BREADE, 30
Allen, 10, 67
BRETT
Robert, 54, 55
BRIANT
William, 46
BRIDGES
Edmond, 45, 66
Edmond R., 66
Mary, 58
Robert, 34, 58
Sarah (___), 66
BRIDGHAM
Elizabeth (___), 6
Jonathan, 6
Joseph, 66
BRIGGS
George, 34
BRIMBLECOM
Phillip, 24
BRITT
Robert, 55
BROME
William, 6
BROWN see also BROWNE
Ephm., 87
Hanna (___), 19
James, 19, 78
William, 39
BROWNE see also BROWN
___, Mr., 21
Abraham, 58
Benjamin, 21, 42, 45
Hana (___), 64
Hana/ Hanna/ Hannah, 64
Hugh, 81
James, 11, 22, 64, 71
John, 37, 55, 61, 64, 70, 71
Nicholas, 1
Richard, 29
Sarah (___), 11
Thomas, 10, 42
William, 1, 10, 16, 20, 21, 27, 45, 48,
  58, 61, 77, 81-83
BROWNING
Thomas, 84
BUCKLEY
William, 29

BUFFAM/BUFFUM
___, Mrs., 18, 28
___, Wid., 4, 6
Caleb, 22
Joshua, 18, 22, 28, 51, 76, 77
Robert, 17
BUKHAM
James, 38
BULLOCK
John, 11
BURNAP
Ann, 46
Robert, 46
BURRILL
John, 47
BURTON
Isaack, 40
John, 21, 64
BUXTON
John, 8

CALDWELL
John, 4
CALEY
John, 37
CAMPBELL
Hugh, 50, 52
CARRILL
Mary (___), 26
Nathaniel, 26
CARTER
Tobias, 41
CASE
Humphry, 32, 33
CAVE
Mary, 43
Thomas, 43
CHADWELL
Moses, 10
CHARD
William, 9
CHEEVERS/CHEEVER
Ezekiell, 11, 30
Peeter/Peter, 20, 35, 50, 51, 76
Samuel, 74
Thomas, 74
CHIN
John, 27, 28
CHUB/CHUBB
Avis (___), 52
Thomas, 15, 52, 60

CLARK/CLARKE/CLEARK/
  CLEARKE
___, Mr., 34
Daniel, 24
Thomas, 22, 46
William, 3, 10
CLEAVES/CLEEVES
George, 31, 32
William, 10
CLIFFORD
John, 13
COAKE
John, 77
COALE
Thomas, 28
COBBETT/COBBITT
___, Mr., 46, 64
Thomas, 63, 64
CODNAM
Robert, 42
CODNER
Cristopher, 38
COE/COES
Grace, 69, 70
Michael, 68-70
COGGSWELL/COGSWELL
John, 5
Margaret (___), 5
COLDUM
Clement, 41, 42
Johanah (___), 41, 42
Mary, 42
Thomas, 41
COLE
Abraham, 37, 45, 46, 49, 76, 77, 82, 83
Ann (___), 37
Sara/Sarah (___), 76, 77
Thomas, 37
COLEBURNE
Henry, 84
COLES
John, 66
COLLENS/COLLINS
James, 5
John, 41
Henry, 29
John, 39
CONANT
___, Mr., 80
John, 9, 14, 15, 59
Roger, 14, 24, 83

CONDY
Samuell, 86
CONRAD
Richard, 68
COOK
Isaack, 21
John, 68
Richard, 72
COOPER
Sarah (___), 53, 54
Thomas, 53, 54
CORBIN
Robert, 31
CORMWELL
Phillip, 45
CORNELL
George, 57
CORWIN
Elizabeth, 30
George, 15, 30, 31, 43, 44, 70
John, 83
Jonathan, 37, 83
COTT, 14
COURSER
William, 72
COWDERY/COWDRY
Nathaniell, 1
William, 1, 46
CRAFORD
Mordecai, 12
CROAD/CROADE/CROADES/
  CROADY
___, Mr., 76
Frances, 27, 49, 50
John, 41
Richard, 5, 18, 27, 37, 49, 50, 54, 59,
  75, 77, 78, 82
CROMWELL
John, 5, 19, 20, 63, 64, 67, 78
Mary (___), 74
Phillip, 5, 18, 19, 28, 39, 45, 63, 64, 66,
  74, 79, 82, 83
CROWE
Christopher, 9
CURTICE/CURTIS
Ephraim, 8
John, 12
Zacheus, 8, 33, 34

DALIBER
Rebecca R., 18

DANFORTH
Jonothan, 73
DARBIE
Roger, 76
DARICH
Michaell, 63
DARLAND
John, 77
Mary (___), 77
DARLING
John, 75, 76
Mary, 75
Mary (___), 76
DAVIS
John, 17, 33, 59
DAY
John, 19
deMARESTON
Adrion, 29
DEAKER
Jokn, 45
DEAN/DEANE
George, 17, 28, 72, 76, 78
Thomas, 78
DERBY
Roger, 77
DEVERIX/DEVORIX
Humphry, 38
John, 38, 74
DEXTER
Thomas, 66
DICER
William, 74
DICKSEY/DICKSIE see DIXY
DIKE
Anthony, 7
Marjery (Pickman), 7
Richard, 17
DIVEN
John, 67
DIXY/DICKSEY/DICKSIE
Anna (___), 70
Thomas, 69, 70
William, 7, 40, 60, 70, 80
DOD
Tho., 29
DODG/DODGE
Joseph, 38
Mary (___), 9
Richard, 37
William, 1, 9, 24, 60, 61

91

FRAILE/FRAYLES
George, 10
Samuel, 10, 29, 30
FREEMAN
John, 86
FREIND
John, 12, 83
Samuell, 83
FRYER
Elizabeth, 17
FULLER
___, Ens., 46
Benjamin, 76
John, 47, 60, 67
Mary (Darling), 76
Thomas, 17, 54
FURBUSH
John, 8
FURSMAN
Arthur, 6

GAGE
Thomas, 77
GALE/GALES
Ambrose, 3, 86
Edmond, 15, 31, 32
Sarah (___), 15
GALLOWAYE
Hugh, 63, 64
GALLY
John, 26
GARDNER
Ebenezer, 7, 35, 37, 50, 56, 57
Elizabeth, 64
George, 2, 4, 13, 30, 35, 56
John, 5
Joseph, 58, 70
Mary (Porter), 13
Samuel, 2, 3, 13, 20, 30, 35, 56-58, 85
Thomas, 1-4, 13, 58
GASFRIGHT
Charles, 71
GASKILL
Edward, 76
Provided, 65
GASKIN
___, Mr., 28
Edward, 49, 82
GATCHELL
Samuel, 29
Thomas, 11, 29

GEDNER
Bartholmew, 13
GEDNEY/GIDNEY
___, Mr., 34, 61
Bartholomew, 3, 16, 39, 43, 76, 78,
    80-82
Eleazer, 25, 37, 55
Hannah (___), 3
John, 3, 11, 38, 58, 83, 85
Susanah, 85
Susanna (___), 3
GEORGE
Richard, 47
GERRISH
Benjamin, 6, 20
GIDDING
Thomas, 24
GIDNEY see GEDNEY
GIFFORD
John, 71
GILBERT
William, 3
GILES
Eleazer, 45, 84
GILL
William, 54
GILLOW
John, 47
GINGELL
John, 16, 17
GLANFIELD
Robert, 7
GODFERY
Johnn, 8
GODSOE
William, 38
GOLD see also GOOLD, GOULD
John, 83
Sarah (___), 83
GOLT
William, 54
GOOD
John, 36
GOODELL, 43
Isaac, 7, 68
Robert, 68
Zachariah, 7, 8
GOOLD see also GOLD, GOULD, 83
John, 12, 84
Sarah, 12
Sarah (___), 84

HEWETT
William, 74
HIBBERT
Robert, 26
HICHINS
Daniell, 34
HIDE/HIDES
Richard, 10, 16, 42
HIGGENSON/HIGGINSON
Henry, 42
John, 1, 12, 13, 15, 23, 35, 39
HILL
John, 21, 30
Zebulon, 18
HOARE
___, Goodman, 46
William, 66, 68
HODGE
Robert, 25, 64
HODGES
Catherine, 56
George, 46, 55, 56
Sarah (___), 46
HOEMAN
Edward, 3
HOLIHOCK
___, Maj., 1
___, Mr., 1
HOLIOAK see HOLYOKE
HOLLINGSWORTH/
HOLLINGWORTH
Richard, 13, 42, 45
William, 13
HOLMES
John, 7
HOLYOKE/HOLIOAK
___, Maj., 46
Elizur, 27
Mary (___), 27
HOOPER
Elizabeth (___), 15
Robert, 7
William, 15
HORNE
___, Deac., 43
Benjamin, 2
Daniell, 72
HOW
John, 84
HOWARD
Samuell, 62

HUBBARD
Richard, 37
Sarah, 37
HUCHENSON/HUCHINSON see also
HUTCHENSON
John, 35
Joseph, 10, 35, 43
Mary, 35
Richard, 35, 36, 49, 50
Sarah (___), 49, 50
HUDD
Richard, 47
HUDSON
John, 11, 28
Mary (___), 28
HUMFRYS/HUMPHREY/
HUMPHREYS/HUMPHREYS/
HUMPHRIES/HUMPHRY/
HUMPHRYES/HUNPHREYE
___, Mr., 3, 34, 62, 63
Edw /Edward, 4, 6, 24, 25, 28, 69, 70
HUTCHENSON/HUTCHESON/
HUTCHINSON see also
HUCHENSON
Edward, 1
John, 43
Joseph, 11

IBROOK
Sarah, 27
INGERSOLL
George, 31
Richard, 10
INGERSON
Nathaniell, 11
IRELAND
William, 16, 17, 51
IVES
Thomas, 18

JACKSON
Jonathan, 39
JAMISON
William, 39
JEGGELLS/JEGGLES
Thomas, 7, 20
William, 7
JENCKES
Joseph, 47
Samuell, 47

JOANES
George, 32
Hugh, 74
JOHNSON
___, Mr., 34
Daniell, 82
Frances, 3, 65, 84
Hanna/ Hannah/ Hanah (___), 3, 65
Samuell, 34, 82
JUXSON
John, 71

**KEASER/KEASON/KEASOR/
KESOR/KEYSER**
Benjamin, 6
Elizer, 6, 30
George, 5, 6, 30, 77, 78
KEMBALL
Charles, 38
KENEY
Henry, 40, 49
Thomas, 49
KESOR/KEYSER see KEASER
KILCUPP/KILLCUPP
Richard, 72
William, 34, 72
KILLUM
Hannah (___), 68
Lott, 7, 68
KING
___, Mr., 22
Charles I I, 71
Daniel, 24, 38, 39, 57
John, 45
Ralph, 22, 38, 39, 65
KIRTLAND
Nathaniell, 59, 62
KITCHIN
John, 21
KNIGHT
Charles, 79
Jacob, 10, 33
Jonathan, 43
Phillip, 43
Richard Combs, 71
Robert, 25
Walter, 79, 80
William, 10
KNIGHTS
Rob't, 84

KNOT/KNOTT
Hannah (___), 11
Richard, 11, 28, 29, 38, 57

LAKE
William, 13
LAMBERT
John, 28, 60
LANE
John, 8
LARCUM
Cornelius, 10
Mordecay, 10
LATTAMORE
___, Mr., 70
Christopher, 27, 48
Mary (___), 48, 49
LAWES, 55
Frances, 44
Francis, 67
LEACH
John, 12, 13, 57, 83
Laurance, 83
Robert, 50
Samuel, 20, 49, 50
Sarah, 13
LEADER, 84
LEB
John, 15
LEGG
___, Mr., 70
___, Mrs., 68
John, 57
LEGROE
John, 29
LEMON
Grace, 74
Mary (___), 74
Robert, 74
LEONARD
Thomas, 47
LEWES
George, 31
John, 31
LEWIS
Ellenor (___), 31, 32
George, 31
John, 31, 32, 67
LINDALL
Timothy, 47

Richard, 53
Thomas, 37, 70
PEACH
John, 84
PEARSON
John, 47
PEASE
John, 2, 21, 26, 27
Nathaniell, 26
PEETERS see PETERS
PENNELTON
Brian, 60, 61
PENSENT
William, 54
PERKINS
David, 59, 60, 68
Elizabeth (___), 60
Thomas, 24
PERSE
Bethia, 45
PERSON
John, 1
PETERS/PEETERS
Hugh, 43, 44
PETHERICK
John, 27
PHILLIP/PHILLIPS
Stainwood, 17
Walter, 57
PHIPPEN
David, 25
PICKERING
John, 11, 16, 44, 75, 76
Jonathan, 75
PICKET/PICKETT
Nicholas, 11, 57
PICKMAN
Marjery, 7
Nathaniel, 7, 25, 48, 85
Samuell, 7
William, 7
PICTON
Thomas, 26
PIKE
George, 86
PILGRIM
John, 48, 70, 71
PINSON
Rebecka (___), 85
William, 85, 86

PITMAN
John, 48
Thomas, 3, 68, 69
PITNAM
Nathanyel, 54, 55
PITT/PITTS
Grace, 48
Susana (___), 48
William, 27, 48
POATE
William, 9
POLAND
James, 16, 50
POLEN/POLIN see also POWLEN
James, 59
John, 36
POPE
___, Wid., 2, 3
Benjamin, 68
Joseph, 21, 68
PORTER
Benjamin, 40
Israel, 6, 34, 73, 85
John, 1, 13, 58, 68
Joseph, 6
Mary, 13
Mary (___), 1, 13, 58
POTTER
Robert, 47
POULTNOY
Richard, 52
POWLAND, 75
POWLEN/POWLLEN/POWLEY see
also POLEN
James, 46, 59, 63, 64, 74
POWLLEN see POWLEN
PREIST see also PRIEST
John, 1, 58
PRESTON
Thomas, 54
PRICE
Eliza (___), 41
Elizabeth (___), 41
John, 41, 55, 57
Mathew, 39, 78
Walter, 9, 41
PRIEST see also PREIST
John, 38
PRINCE
Richard, 84
Samuell, 84

99

Thomas, 18
PRISCOTT
Peeter, 43
PROVENDER
John, 62
PUDEATER
Ann/Anne (___), 50, 51
Jacob, 50, 51
PUDNEY
John, 21, 62, 63
PUTNAM/PUTTNAM
Edward, 43
Elizabeth, 36
John, 11, 17, 40, 86
Jonathan, 40
Nathanell, 55
Nathaniel, 18, 19, 34, 36, 55
Thomas, 34-36, 39, 43, 73, 86

RAMSDELL
Aquila, 46, 47
Isaac, 47
John, 46, 47
RAMSON
Edw., 72
RAYMENT
John, 9, 60, 61
William, 60, 61
REA
Joshua, 60, 85
REDFORD
Charles, 1, 10, 46, 77
REDINGTON
Abraham, 8
REDKNAP
Joseph, 47
REEVE/REEVES
William, 63, 64
RENOLDS/REYNOLDS
Henry, 17-19, 22
RIALL, 12
RICE
Jno, 6
RICH
Bethiah, 41
RICHARDS
Ann (___), 22, 33
Daniell, 33
Edward, 22, 33
John, 22, 46, 53

RICHARDSON
Amose, 48
RIDDAN/RIDDEN
___, Mr., 38
Elizabeth., 28
Thaddeus, 6, 27, 29
RIGGS
Thomas, 18
RING
John, 20, 21
ROADES/ROADS
Henry, 29, 30, 62
Samuell, 62
ROBBINS
Mary (___), 85
Thomas, 17, 25, 76, 77, 82, 85, 86
ROBBISSON see ROBISSON
ROBINSON
John, 25, 31, 33, 34
Thos., 28
ROBISSON/ROBBISSON
John, 20
Martha (___), 20
Samuel, 20
Sarah (___), 20
William, 20
ROBSON
John, 71
ROGERS
John, 23
ROOTE
Catherine (___), 55
ROOTEN
Anna (___), 82
Richard, 82
ROOTES
Josiah, 9, 46, 60
Katharen (___), 46
Thomas, 46, 55, 56
ROSE
Killecrus, 20
ROUNDY
Robert, 59
ROWLESES
___, Mr., 47
ROYAL/ROYALL, 14, 83
RUBTON
John, 13
RUCK
Abigall, 79
Elizabeth, 55, 79

Ellenor, 68
Ellenor (___), 69, 70
John, 68
STAINWOOD
___, Goodman, 17
STANDISH
James, 49, 50
STANLIE/STANLY/STANLYE, 84
Caleb, 56
George, 70
Mathew, 83, 85
Samuell, 83
STEEVENS
John, 41
STILEMAN
Elias, 31, 66, 84, 85
STOCKER
Ebenezer, 67
STONE, 29
John, 15, 59
Nathaniell, 10
Remember (___), 10
Robert, 2, 15
STORY
___, Goodman, 5
SWASY/SWAZY
Jo., 82
Joseph, 76, 77
SWEATLAND/SWETLAND
William, 51, 66
SWEET
Robert, 29
SWETLAND see SWEATLAND
SWINERTON, 49
Job, 21, 40
John, 2, 3, 31
SYMONDS
James, 37, 43

TAILER/TAILOR see also TAYLER
Edward, 1
TALEY
Richard, 64
TAMLY
John, 72
TAPLEY
Gilbert, 12, 26
TARBOX
Samuell, 10
TARVIS
Andrew, 46

Sarah (___), 46
TAYLER/TAYLOR see also TAILER
Edward, 1
Elizabeth (___), 1
THISSELL
Richard, 40
THOMAS
David, 14
George, 86
THOMPSON
Benjamin, 8
THORNETON
Timothy, 51
TOD/TODD/TODE
John, 8
TOMLIN/TOMLINS
Edward, 58, 65
TOPPAN
Jacob, 36
TOWNE
Joseph, 12
TOWNSEND
John, 1
Thomas, 59
TRAPP
Thomas, 39
TRASK/TRASKE, 30
Elizabeth (___), 53
John, 32, 33, 59
William, 32, 33
TREBEE
John, 6
TREVETT/TREVIT/TREVITTS
Henry, 29, 57
John, 11
TRICKER
Marke, 38
TUCK
Joane (___), 9
Thomas, 9, 55
TURNER
John, 2, 23, 65

UPTON
John M., 68
USHER
Hezekiah, 71

VEREN
Dorcas, 66
Hannah, 27

102

Hillard, 2-8, 11-14, 16-20, 22, 25, 27,
   29-31, 34, 39, 41, 43-45, 48, 49, 51,
   55, 66, 68, 71-75, 77, 78, 84
   Joshua, 33
   Nathaniel, 43
   Phillip, 12, 17, 84
VERRY/VERRYE/VERY/VERYE
   Alce (___), 18
   Hanah (___), 41
   Samuel, 18, 32, 33, 45, 84
   Thomas, 41
   Samuell, 33

WAITE
   Gemaliek, 48
   John, 23
WAKEFIELD
   Samuell, 68
WAKELIN/WAKELINE
   Luke, 24
WAKELY
   John, 32
WALCUTT/WALLCUTT see also
   WOOLCOT
   Abraham, 7
   Jonathan, 10, 11, 14
WALKER
   Richard, 57
   Rich'd, 57
WALLCUTT see WALCUTT
WALLER
   Christopher, 78
WALLINGFORD
   Nicholas, 36
WALLIS
   Bartho., 32
   Margarett (___), 31, 32
   Nathaniell, 9, 15, 31, 32
WALTON
   Nathaniell, 28, 74
   William, 83
WARD
   Peter, 65
   Samuell, 49, 86
WARREN
   Abraham, 14
WATERS
   Richard, 31
WATSON
   Thomas, 51

WATTS
   Jeremiah, 85
WAYE
   William, 17
WAYES
   Aron, 17
WEBB
   ___, Mr., 54
   Bridged, 79
WELCH
   Phillip, 74
WELD
   Daniell, 45, 51
WELLS
   Nathaniell, 21
WELMAN
   Thomas, 46
WEST
   Elizabeth, 55
   Elizabeth (___), 55
   Henry, 34, 55
   Samuell, 9, 14, 15, 53
   William, 23, 73
WHARTON
   Edmund, 66
   Edward, 31, 84
WHEELER
   Thomas, 47, 60
WHITE
   ___, Mr., 81
   Abigail (___), 40, 41, 75
   Elias, 29, 57
   John, 37, 42
   Josiah, 75
   Remember (___), 75
   Resolved, 40, 41, 75
   Thomas, 36, 37
   Zachariah, 19
WHITFORD
   Bridgett (___), 78, 79
   Walter, 78, 79
WHITING
   John, 30
   Samuell, 62
WHITNED
   Thomas, 62
WHITRIG
   Thomas, 68
WHITTINGHAM
   ___, Mr., 61

WILKASON/WILKENSON/
  WILKENSON/WILKINSON
Abraham, 62
Bray, 17
Isaac, 62
John, 62
Jon, 47
WILKES
Robert, 23
WILKINSON see WILKASON
WILLIAMS
Isaac, 67
Jane (___), 8, 9
John, 8, 9, 15, 51, 71
William, 14
WILLOSSES
___, Mr., 47
WILLOUGHBY
Nehemiah, 25, 48, 77
WILSON
Edward, 42
Robert, 4, 27
WINTER
Josiah, 22
WITT/WITTS
John, 67
Jon., 10
WOLLAN
Edward, 73
WOOD
Anthony, 14, 23, 53, 59
Thomas, 23
William, 9
WOODBERRY/WOODBERY/
  WOODBERYE/WOODBURY/
  WOODBURYE
Andrew, 74, 79
Hugh, 1, 40, 53
Humphry, 81
Isaake, 24
John, 24, 80, 81
Nicholas, 40
Richard, 52
WOODBRIDG/WOODBRIDGE
Thomas, 36
WOODBURY/WOODBURYE see
  WOODBERRY
WOODWELL
Mathew, 55
WOODY
Eliezer, 52

WOOLCOT see also WALCUTT
Mary, 41
WOOLEN
Edward, 19
WOOLINGFORD
Nicholas, 36
WOOLLAM
Edward, 73

104

www.ingramcontent.com/pod-product-compliance
Lightning Source LLC
Chambersburg PA
CBHW071059090426
42737CB00013B/2384